a child's work

a child's work

THE IMPORTANCE OF FANTASY PLAY

vivian gussin paley

The University of Chicago Press
Chicago and London

VIVIAN GUSSIN PALEY, a kindergarten and nursery school teacher for thirty-seven years, primarily at the University of Chicago Laboratory Schools, has received numerous awards and accolades, including a MacArthur Award and most recently the John Dewey Society's Outstanding Achievement Award. She is the author of eleven books, three of which are published by the University of Chicago Press.

The University of Chicago Press, Chicago 60637
The University of Chicago Press, Ltd., London
© 2004 by The University of Chicago
All rights reserved. Published 2004
Printed in the United States of America

13 12 11 10 09 08 07 06 05 04   1 2 3 4 5
ISBN: 0-226-64487-1 (cloth)

Library of Congress Cataloging-in-Publication Data

Paley, Vivian Gussin, 1927–
    A child's work : the importance of fantasy play / Vivian Gussin Paley.
      p. cm.
    ISBN 0-226-64487-1 (cloth : alk. paper)
    1. Play.   2. Early childhood education.   I. Title.

LB1139.35.P55P35 2004
155.4'18—dc22

                                            2003066281

♾ The paper used in this publication meets the minimum requirements of the American National Standard for Information Sciences—Permanence of Paper for Printed Library Materials, ANSI Z39.48-1992.

God created Man
because He loves stories.

ELIE WIESEL

contents

a child's work

one
young children

The first time I heard that "play is the work of children" was in 1949 from Rena Wilson, director of the Newcomb Nursery School in New Orleans. She was describing her "Introduction to Young Children" course at Sophie Newcomb College.

As a newly arrived senior in the college, I was completing the undergraduate studies I had interrupted by getting married and moving to New Orleans. I hadn't yet decided to become a teacher but it seemed a good idea to learn something about little children, and Miss Wilson promised us a view into the very heart of early childhood.

After the children went home, our class sat on the child-sized chairs in the nursery school, our minds still puzzling over what we had observed there earlier in the day. Miss Wilson had told us, "You are watching the only age group in school that is always busy making up its own work assignments. It looks and sounds like play, yet we properly call this play the work of children. Why? That is what you are here to find out."

None of us thought the task was easy. As soon as we

began to record one set of events, our subjects were off pretending something else, giving each other information and clues we often could not decipher. But we collected anecdotes, samples of conversation, sketches of block constructions, and drippy paintings and tried to see what the children were learning. What we couldn't capture was the intensity and intentionality that accompanied everything the children said and did—until Miss Wilson gently persuaded us to add our imagination to the mix.

"Pretend *you* are the children who are playing," she said. "What are you trying to accomplish and what stands in your way? Act out what you've seen and fill in the blanks. Remind yourselves of what it was like to be a child."

In time we discovered that play was indeed work. First there was the business of deciding who to be and who the others must be and what the environment is to look like and when it is time to change the scene. Then there was the even bigger problem of getting others to listen to *you* and accept *your* point of view while keeping the integrity of the make-believe, the commitment of the other players, and perhaps the loyalty of a best friend. Oddly enough, the hardest part of the play for us to reproduce or invent were the fantasies themselves. Ours were never as convincing or interesting as the children's; it took us a great deal of practice to do what was, well, child's play in the nursery.

More than fifty years have passed since Rena Wilson led her children and their teachers plus several generations of college students in the daily celebration of play. What would she make of today's revision of priorities in our nation's early childhood centers and kindergartens, where lessons have begun to replace play as the center-piece of community life?

"Is it possible," she might ask, "that *work* is now the play of children? No, this will never do. We must begin again, to watch and listen to the children. We have forgotten what it is like to be a child."

We will need to go beyond watching, listening, and re-membering, however, if our children are to be revealed as the same original thinkers and actors they were in Rena Wilson's day. In documenting and dramatizing their lan-guage, lore, and literary strivings, my purpose is to exam-ine their curriculum in its natural form, much as they study one another through the medium of their play.

If my narrative travels back and forth between genera-tions, it is because this fantasy play remains amazingly constant. The children you will meet in Nisha Ruparel-Sen's kindergarten are little different from those I taught in the same school thirty years earlier. They and all the others whose play and stories inform these pages continue to be the most innovative researchers I know in answering Miss Wilson's question: Why do we call play the work of young children?

Furthermore, why not call play the work of teachers as well? If, as Lev Vygotsky, the Russian psychologist, in-forms us, children rise above their average behavior in play, let us pursue the ways in which their teachers might follow them up the ladder, starting at the first rung, which, as every child knows, is fantasy play.

two
the language of play

There was a time when play was king and early childhood was its domain. Fantasy was practiced leisurely and openly in a language unique to the kingdom. It is still spoken in Mrs. Ruparel-Sen's kindergarten.

"Ahzz! Water, water! Pretend we are walking in Egypt and there's no water but we see a big river."

"Gulp, gulp, gulp, come on, drink it!"

"No, I'm drowning. Help, help! Wait, there's a huge bullfrog jumping. Higher than the World Trade Center! He can't stay alive. There's no bugs to eat there any more. Hey, what's going on!"

"It's exploding! Jump away, hurry. Jump in the river. The bullfrog is on fire. Come on, we gotta swim fast. Get away from the fire. Swim faster! Whew! I saved you!"

The children swimming to safety, away from the exploding bullfrog, have begun a conversation about the World Trade Center tragedy.

Vijay, from India, is newly arrived in Mrs. Ruparel-Sen's class. He has not yet begun to play with other children, but he listens to their fantasy play in the blocks, murmuring to the toy airplane he circles around himself at the edge of the block area.

"Hey, you wanna bomb us?" asks the blond boy who is rebuilding the tower of blocks that has just exploded. It seems a gracious invitation but Vijay shakes his head, not ready to take direct action. There is another way in this classroom to enter the culture of the community and the world of childhood. He sits down at the story table.

"I have a story," Vijay says softly, surprising his teacher, who sits at a table writing down the stories children dictate to her. This is the first time Vijay has offered to tell a story without her encouragement. His story has no other outlet at school since he did not tell it to the tower builder in the blocks. He might have waited until he got home but perhaps there would be no one there ready to listen. Clearly he could not wait; his story must be told now and the words tumble out.

"This was a plane," he begins. "Then it went to O'Hare and it picked up my grandpa last year. And my grandma was at Madras and then she went to India and we went to the Westin Hotel building. And the plane crashed into O'Hare. And into the Westin tall building. And then they fixed the plane and they had to fix all the people. And they were going home. But they couldn't fix the building. It was on fire."

Mrs. Ruparel-Sen gives Vijay a solemn look. "Who will you be when we act out your story?" she asks. In this class the dictated story is but a half-told tale. To fulfill its destiny it is dramatized on a pretend stage with the help of classmates as actors and audience and the teacher as narrator and director.

"The airplane," Vijay says, rolling his toy back and forth

on the table. He waits a moment, then adds, "Do you know what Vijay means? It means victory."

"Vijay means victory? I'm glad you told me that." Mrs. Ruparel-Sen needs more information. "Will we see the plane being fixed? And the people too?"

"Yes," Vijay says. "How do you say the fixers?"

"Mechanics?" the teacher suggests.

He nods. "And a doctor for the people. And the ambulance. And the firemen too. But not a loud noise."

Mrs. Ruparel-Sen writes down the additional directions. "Victory," she repeats. "When the people go home in your story, it's another victory."

Kostos has been moving a tiny superhero figure next to Vijay's paper. "You need T-Rex in your story?" he asks. "He's a victory too, I'm pretty sure." Vijay shakes his head but the boys stare silently at the doll that has the power of a dinosaur.

Kostos knows Vijay's subject matter. He is from Greece and, like Vijay, has many relatives who fly to America frequently and stay in tall hotels. Kostos is better able to place a fictional character between himself and the crash, perhaps because he has more practice in the doll corner and block areas, where questions and explanations are worked out dramatically every day.

When it is his turn to dictate a story, Kostos picks up his classmate's theme, as though they are having a conversation. "Once a airplane was going too fast with people in it. Then T-Rex came. He jumped up and down and the airplane crashed into him but he is much stronger. Then the people jump out on T-Rex's head. And he shakes the people off into the water because they can swim fast. Then they fall asleep and their jackets are pillows."

Props are seldom used in Mrs. Ruparel-Sen's class when stories are acted out but when the T-Rex story is dramatized, the children performing in it run to get their jackets, which they fold carefully into pillows. It is a moment of theater when words are unnecessary. A conversation has begun about the events of September 11th that will weave through the children's stories and fantasy play. Grownups may speak often of that terrible time and there will be repeated reports and replays on television, but the children must be able to imagine themselves swimming to safety and using their jackets as pillows.

For the next several days, the children reenact aspects of Vijay's and Kostos's stories. Whatever the plot, there is a plane crash and the children bring their jackets. By the following week, Vijay is now the grandfather in the doll corner, with thoughts of plane crashes set aside.

What an astonishing invention is this activity we call fantasy play. Are we really willing to let it disappear from our preschools and kindergartens? "I'm not inclined to encourage fantasy play any more if my teachers can't handle it," a preschool director admitted recently. "If the teachers are worried about what's coming out, especially with the fours and fives, everyone is better off if we stick to lesson plans and projects."

"Has the play changed that much?" I asked.

"The teachers think so. Maybe it's the increased tension since 9/11. Children do seem less prepared, more at risk. We're on safer ground with a somewhat academic curriculum. It's more dependable."

I would have to disagree. There is no activity for which young children are better prepared than fantasy play. Nothing is more dependable and risk-free, and the dangers are only pretend. What we are in danger of doing is delegitimatizing mankind's oldest and best-used learning tool.

In the pages that follow, my attention to fantasy play may appear to overwhelm the many other areas of exploration in a preschool and kindergarten. I would not do without the books we read and reread until they are memorized; the arts, crafts, and games we make and remake as we enlarge our perspectives and skills; and the music and poetry that give rhythm and rhyme to our feelings.

However, since fantasy play is the glue that binds together all other pursuits, including the early teaching of reading and writing skills, I am compelled to put it on display as clearly as I can. A former editor of mine always asked: What is the focus of your book and where is the growth? The spotlight here will be upon the dramatic play of young children, but the growth I attempt to record may well be my own.

It is in the development of their themes and characters and plots that children explain their thinking and enable us to wonder who we might become as their teachers. If fantasy play provides the nourishing habitat for the growth of cognitive, narrative, and social connectivity in young children, then it is surely the staging area for our common enterprise: an early school experience that best represents the natural development of young children.

three
charlotte and cinderella

An incident in a long-ago kindergarten of mine offers an in-progress view of this common enterprise, an investigation of ideas and feelings in conversation, play, and story. Twenty years later, I overhear a consideration of similar issues in Mrs. Ruparel-Sen's doll corner. But first, my class:

"Why does Charlotte?" five-year-old Adam asked as I put down *Charlotte's Web* at the end of chapter 9.

"Why does she what?"

"What *is* she?"

"Do you mean is she a spider?"

"How does she do that?"

"Spin a web?" I asked.

"No, to Wilbur."

"Talk to him?"

"Why is she his friend?" The question has emerged.

"Oh, that. I've also wondered about that," I replied, beginning to formulate my answer. But Adam was ready with his own explanation.

"Because she loves him. And she's lonely for her baby.

The baby is gone, growed up, and now she has Wilbur. That's why."

Adam already had a reputation for being rough on the playground, grabbing boys and pulling them down. Yet he knows why Charlotte is Wilbur's friend. After my conversation with Adam, I noticed him in the doll corner arranging blankets into a nest-like pile. "This is for Wilbur," he said. "Jenny is Charlotte. She's my mother."

"You'll be safe and comfortable in this nest. But where is Charlotte?" I asked.

He pointed to the easel. "She has to paint the web for us."

Are the fives too old for such play? Is it too "babyish" for children who are supposed to be preparing for first grade? At the story table Jennie provided "proof" that such play is what children still need and put to good use. "There was a baby pig named Wilbur," she dictated. "Then came a spider and she hears him crying in the barn. 'Don't cry, because you and me is our family.' And they are best friends."

Jennie and Adam, in play and story, had captured the essence of E. B. White's masterpiece. Speaking of Wilbur and Charlotte near the end of the book, the author writes, "No one had ever had such a friend—so affectionate, so loyal, and so skillful."

"What's skillful?" Jennie asked, after her story was acted out.

"Doing something very well," I answered.

"Oh yeah, Wilbur is skillful 'cause Charlotte puts 'terrific' in the web."

"Or maybe Charlotte is skillful because she knows how to write 'terrific' in the web," I said.

"Both has to be skillful," Adam concluded, "and both has to be best friends." Every child in the class understood that *Charlotte's Web* is an extraordinary tale of friendship and love, skills that are practiced in the doll corner, the blocks, and even on the playground, cumbersome as that sometimes appears to the outsider when these skills are mixed into a Spiderman scenario. The children do not ask themselves whether Wilbur is immature or whether Charlotte acts enough like a spider. E. B. White himself would think the children's play correctly reflects the relationship between Wilbur and Charlotte, as complex and mature a concept as we could possibly introduce.

Mrs. Ruparel-Sen, as it happens, has also been reading *Charlotte's Web* to the children, chapter by chapter, after lunch as I once did. During the playtime that follows, "Charlotte" runs into the doll corner shouting, "Where's Wilbur. Hide him! They're coming!"

"I'm Fern. I'll do it."

"No, it hasta be Charlotte. C'mon, Wilbur, you're my baby. Get in the crib quick."

"He's my baby too, okay? Pretend we're sisters."

"Okay, but I'm the big sister. Charlotte hasta be the big sister."

If readiness for school has meaning, it is to be found first in the children's flow of ideas, their own and those of their peers, families, teachers, books, and television, from play into story and back into more play. It was when I asked the children to dictate their stories and bring them to life again on a stage that the connections between play and analytical thinking became clear. The children and I were nourishing the ground and opening the seed packets, ready to plant our garden of ideas and identities.

One such seed packet could be labeled "Charlotte and Wilbur" and another "Cinderella." In my own kindergarten, after a second reading of *Cinderella* I could see that the doll-corner players were preparing the soil for the *idea* of Cinderella.

"Scrub the floor, Cinderella! You can't come to the ball."

"Then you don't come to the birthday."

"Whose birthday?"

"Me. I'm baby Cinderella. And there's no mean sisters so you can't act mean to me. You could be a nice sister or a good auntie."

If Charlotte and Wilbur encourage the children to act out issues of friendship and safety, then Cinderella, it seems, adds the equally important question of power to the mix. The doll-corner players warn the stepsisters not to be mean and risk missing the birthday party. Then they change Cinderella into a baby to see if this role gives her more power. But even babies require further preparation:

"Now I'm the tiny baby and you're the big sister."

"We could be both two sisters and the baby isn't borned."

"We need a dad then. Billy, are you the dad? You hafta say, 'Where's the baby?' and I hafta say, 'She's not borned yet.'"

"Where's the baby?"

"She's not borned yet. She's getting out of her mother in one day."

"Then one day is over. I hear her crying."

The children moved from one strong emotion to the next, briefly noting its dimensions: from pleasure to jealousy, from power to abandonment to recovery, observing each resolution and analyzing the total effect. If only playtime could last longer, they must think, then every character could be forewarned and vindicated. In so doing the children stretch their language and logic beyond our expectations.

"Sh-sh! The baby is crying under a mushroom."

"I'm the good fairy to take her to the ball."

"When she's older, you mean. We didn't finish babies yet. And the dad isn't the prince now. That hasta be later."

"The dad could be a superhero later too, don't forget."

Which comes first, Cinderella who sits by the ashes, the one who goes to the ball, or the baby under the mushroom? Lily, who enjoyed being Baby Cinderella, knew what happened in the fairy tale. But she was not ready to take on a mature role. At the story table she said, "There is a baby called Cinderella. But she's too little for the ball. Her mother brings her to the park."

Closure was not the goal for Lily when there were still so many ideas to be put into words. In the same mood, the boys at the sand table tried to figure out why a mother pig would send her children to live in a dangerous forest. Or, more precisely, why did she send the baby brother away?

"Here's where the mother pig lives. In this hole."

"The baby pig wants to come in. Let me in!"

"No babies, Warren. She's too old. She wants to be by herself."

"Then she can't be a mother."

"Not by herself to the baby! To the brothers to go away! She locks the door on those guys."

"Okay, just the baby pig stays with the mom. And we got all the bricks, right?"

In how many ways can one retell the mother-loves-me-best story? What are the most effective ways to eliminate older siblings? If you find a friend, then are the woods no longer deep and dark? "There was a lonely deer—or rabbit or little boy—and then a friend comes," begin so many stories the children tell, even into first and second grade. No wonder Wilbur's salvation is understood so well. "Once there was a lonely, frightened pig and then came a spider named Charlotte."

When we furnish our early childhood centers with workbooks and computers, will there still be time for the mother pig to reconsider the decision to send her children into the scary woods? And how will Cinderella know the joys of being with the good mother before the unaccountably wicked one appears?

The narrative begins early. Even before the spoken word, the pictures in the young child's mind assume a storylike quality. How else could the dramatic play emerge so fully formed, filling up the spaces in other people's stories? Our books and conversations work their magic because the children meet us more than halfway. They have already begun feeling the emotional highs and lows of the hero and victim and are ready to climb to the next rung of the ladder.

"Did you know *Peter Rabbit* used to be the *Runaway Bunny?*"

"You think it's the same character?"

"It *is* the same. Only Peter is older."

"He does seem older. His mother isn't always looking for him now."

"That's why Peter gets into trouble too much. With Mr. McGregor. I don't like that part."

"But you want me to read it."

"Yeah. I just want to hear it. Because it's in my head now. So I wanna see how it sounds."

four
the first rungs of the ladder

Nearly everything in my training as a teacher led me to believe that the questions were supposed to come from me. Preoccupied by my own questions, I did not perceive that the books I so eagerly read to the children were not the only or even the primary source of stories in the classroom. The children were, in fact, natural-born storytellers who created literature as easily as I turned the pages of a book.

It was not that I doubted the children's seriousness, but I did not follow their words as I would those of a novelist or a playwright. The Brontës must have rehearsed similar themes as they played on the moors of west Yorkshire, yet I gave no thought to such possibilities. I could see that the children's play promoted a long list of social, emotional, verbal, and physical skills that could be reported in a fairly straightforward manner. However, I skipped over the end result, a phenomenon not as easy to capture on a checklist. The children were inventing stories that sounded as if they came from an earlier place in the common narrative, from the first rungs on the ladder of storytelling.

"Pretend I'm your baby dinosaur and I'm lost," a child

might say, "and then you call me but I don't come because I have a different name now and then you hear a noise and you think it's a wolf but you can't call me because you don't know my name now."

This child knows how to play, I would note. She is able to include other children and thus be a friend. But I would pass over the story the child had imagined and the questions of identity being posed. Furthermore, the previous day it may have been the mother dinosaur who was lost and the baby who searched. Roles were constantly being switched and stories unraveled and reissued in different forms, but I confused the extraordinary with the mundane.

Even when I overheard conversations that were startling and profound I seldom recognized the uniqueness of this activity that so preoccupied the children. "Pretend I'm a big sister just like you," said a little girl, climbing out of a doll-corner crib. "I'm not a baby anymore. I'm you!"

"No! Don't pretend that!" cautioned her playmate, suddenly remorseful, stepping out of her role. "Don't be like me! Because I'm really bad!"

"Like the wolf?"

"Oh, wait, now it's okay. I'm a good sister now."

Had I not heard these lines before? Isn't this what the older brother warns the younger brother in *Long Day's Journey Into Night*? Watch out for me, Eugene O'Neill has Jamie tell Edmond, I'm no good and I'll try to bring you down to where I am. But I'm being a good brother now to tell you this.

You have a right to object: Can one really make so much of doll-corner talk? At one time I might have protested myself. Even when I became curious about the substance of the endless conversations carried on as the children played, I still did not grasp the literary dimensions of their spontaneous dialogues. Nor did I wonder why the children were usually more interested in each other's responses than in anything I read to them from a book.

"Are you bad like the stepsister and I can't go to the ball?"
    "Pretend I'm your real mother and I stay home and play with you."

Had I listened more closely I would have heard, among other secrets, that when one is young almost every story begins with and returns to a mother and child. Since I had my own fantasies of being a storyteller, I would have done well to follow some of the themes repeated by the children in their play. I had no illusions of becoming a Beatrix Potter or an E. B. White, but saw my role as a spinner of little tales, the sort that would make me a more interesting teacher or make teaching more interesting to me.

I lacked the spontaneity that might bridge those awkward transitions when our connections to each other are blurred and even the most familiar book or song doesn't cut through the loneliness and restlessness of school days.

The children jumped easily into these voids. They resurrected earlier disguises ("Now I'm Batman and you be Joker") or they corrected injustices ("You always get to be Batman and I never am!"). When nothing more dramatic came to mind, they maintained contact by grabbing at one another, anything to keep connections alive.

These were not the links I coveted, yet the children and

I shared similar goals: to use fantasy to calm our anxieties and reassemble ourselves along promising paths, skipping along together like Dorothy and her new friends in *The Wizard of Oz*. My stories, however, felt awkward and forced, not in rhythm with the children's themes.

I rarely paused to listen to the narratives blooming everywhere in the garden of children in which I spent my days. I saw myself as the bestower of place and belonging, of custom and curriculum, too often ignoring the delicate web being constructed by the children in their constant exchange of ideas the moment I stopped talking and they resumed playing.

"Pretend I'm the good mother."

"Is there a mean one?"

"The step one? No, only one mother, the nice one."

"Let's both be baby sisters and our nice mother isn't lost yet."

"Was she lost or are we lost?"

"Not yet. No one is lost. This is the part where we're still happy."

What can this mean, "the part where we're still happy"? Do the children envision a Garden of Eden and is this what they try to recreate in their play? If only I could return to that doll-corner scene and ask the players what they meant. Their responses would have made an elegant conversation. These were the dialogues that had begun to fill my journals and there was never enough time to follow every intriguing notion and original idea. But it was clear that the children knew it was up to them to begin each day's narrative.

five

the invention of theater

The director of an early childhood center asked in a recent letter, "Where has the dramatic play gone? My teachers claim it is too hard and they shy away from it. They like to plan projects, which do have a place, but which are somehow disconnected from where the children are. They keep interrupting the curriculum the children have for themselves. I've started bringing my tape recorder into the classrooms so I can get down some of this hidden curriculum to study with my staff."

In the 1970s, after many years of teaching, I too began to use a tape recorder in order to listen more carefully to what the children said. Before long, the transcriptions resembled stage directions.

"Pretend you're reading Red Riding Hood," Jilly says, handing me the book.

"Not really reading?"

"No, pretend you're really reading and I'm really pretending." Later, in the doll corner, Jilly explains herself further.

"You be the mother," she tells Cora. "You have to come with me in case there's a wolf."

"First we see the hunter," Cora decides. "He already banged at the wolf."

"But you didn't tell me don't talk to the wolf!"

"No, see, this is the first real way it goes. The wolf sees the mother and so he runs away."

When Jilly asked me to pretend to read *Little Red Riding Hood* she was anticipating what was to take place in the doll corner. She and Cora would not merely copy a familiar tale but would be imagining a piece of theater that precedes the printed version. For the next several days they experimented with flashbacks and fast-forwards, including an episode in which Red Riding Hood is a baby whose very bossy mother does not allow her to go into the forest.

"No no no, Baby Red! You're too young for a forest! Lie down in your crib!"

This particular class, which I described in *Bad Guys Don't Have Birthdays* (1988), spent a good part of the year reinventing characters as babies. There were Baby Superman, Baby He-Man, and Baby Skeletor, in addition to Baby Red Riding Hood and Baby Cinderella. It was a rare hero who was not transformed into a baby.

Why would one group of children devote so much time to baby superheroes? I had recently seen a production of Bernard Shaw's *Man and Superman* in which the birth of a future hero is longingly anticipated. Once again, I was struck by the common wellspring shared by great works of literature and children's fantasy play. Their recent past as babies and their present fantasies of superhero status meet in a variety of imagined roles.

Whatever pattern a small group within a class developed in its play, it took time to spread the word that something new was happening. However, if the ideas could be incorporated into a dictated story, acted out before the entire class, then the sense of full participation came across.

In play it might sound like this: "See, now Superman is just starting so everyone is always surprised. Like we say, 'Oh, I didn't know I could fly!' Like that, okay?"

Translated into theater, the narrative could be slowed down. "Once there was Baby Superman and his mother told him not to crawl because pretty soon he'd be flying. But he said, 'I'll just crawl until I get bigger.'"

Soon the story was ready to be propelled by a new plot device. "Give me the magic potion to make me fly," one could hear on the playground. "No, wait, first you give me the *wrong* potion and I die and then you find the right one and I come alive."

The debate over details seemed endless, which is the point made by a friend who teaches a class that combines kindergarten and first grade. "Whenever I have to concentrate on reading with the sixes," she writes, "the highly imaginative curriculum devised by the fives suffers through lack of time. Good play and the sort of talk that follows take time and deep thought. There are no shortcuts. The early practicing of reading is not a good trade-off, in my view. I'd prefer to keep the fives and their special social curriculum alone."

Her emphasis on "social curriculum" interested me. For although I have long followed the dramatic personae of classroom theater, the drama is not disconnected from the distinctive social imperative played out on the kindergarten stage. Here the children have a clear view, for the first time, of the pecking order in school society. For these insights and others, the kindergarten year can be an exceptionally productive period, the culmination of years of early social observations and fantasy play. By kindergarten, children have the added patience, experience, and vocabulary with which to carry the plot and the characters to places they have never been before, and to apply what they now know to their social relationships.

The children in my kindergarten, for example, in order to help Erik avoid the bad guy role in the doll corner, create a dad hunter who is bitten by a wolf and becomes wolf-like in strength.

"Someone has to be the wolf," Red Riding girl said, putting on the red velvet cloak.

"I'm not the bad guy," argued Erik, in a vest and tie.

"You're really the dad hunter but you pretend huge teeth."

"Like a wolf? See it bited me so my teeth got stronger like a wolf."

Months later I heard about a movie with a similar plot and called Erik's mother. "No, I'm sure Erik doesn't know a thing about the movie," she said. "He's not been to any movies yet and we don't have a television set."

When I described Erik's doll-corner character with teeth, "stronger like a wolf," she laughed. "He's quite fanciful on his own. We read 'Jack and the Beanstalk' to him and his sister last night and right away Erik changes the story to be about a giant's wife and her baby who grows up to be a good giant after he kills the bad giant. When I suggested that he do the story without the killing part, he answered with a bravado we're not used to. 'No can do,' he said. Does that come from school?"

"Probably it does. It's the children's curriculum, you know."

Does it matter if children do not spend time, as Erik and his sister do, playing up and down the fantasy ladder? Could we not just read the storybook and organize a dramatization, handing out roles to play? Is there a difference when children play out their own interpretations and then evolve them further as classroom theater?

Questions such as these can fuel a teacher's curiosity and personal research, for the answers are printed nowhere. They can be found only in the individual classroom as children invent the process and the teacher acts the part of the Greek chorus and amanuensis.

"Erik, before, when you had teeth as strong as a wolf, did you become a different person?" I asked.

"I wasn't too strong," Erik said. "I was only a little bit too strong. A dad can't be that strong except sometimes he can." These are philosophical issues and, as is the case with most serious theater, are subject to reinterpretation whenever the role is played.

"Anyway, I was only pretending, you know." He looks at me quizzically.

"Oh, sure, I know. I meant did you become a pretend different person?" It is clear that my question struck a false note, reminding me that we are always on the periphery of the child's world. Yet our clumsiness is forgiven by the children when they see that we respect their play enough to wonder what happens next.

six
looking for peter rabbit

Although Mr. McGregor waits for Peter in the garden and the wolf is huffing at the door, teachers show a growing preference for the more passive responses elicited by a skills-first curriculum. Children are placed in a quandary: When play is curtailed, how are they to confront their fantasy villains? The potential novelists in our midst are endlessly hampered in the name of readiness for first grade and, increasingly, for kindergarten.

Rena Wilson was never as critical of the young as we have become. Today we judge or prejudge every shade of difference between children. We scrutinize their responses according to arbitrary scales that seldom include the unfolding of children's imaginations as revealed in their play. Nonetheless, the children continue to place their questions in story form for one another's pleasure and information and play out their mini-narratives as if on a stage.

"Where is Peter? I think Mr. McGregor's gonna cook him in a rabbit pie."

"No you don't! Hojah! Bam! I got 'em!"

"Are you a ninja?"

"Just to scare him. I'm still Peter. But I jumped higher than the moon. To a rainbow. You can hide inside the colors. There's a ladder in there."

Children are intoxicated by the seemingly endless supply of plots available just for the thinking. Making up stories is the skill most admired by other children, who do not doubt the value of characters who jump higher than the moon during school time.

"Superman goes higher than the rainbow! Higher than the whole world. Hey, listen to this. Higher than the *school,* that's the *rule.*" On the way to the library the children bounce along with their new images of Superman flying over the school. "Higher than the world, higher than the school, that's just the rule, the rule of the school!"

A stern look from the librarian stops Superman in midflight, but the children now are ready to listen to her story, more so than they would have been if they had been walking silently in lockstep down the hall. The mind that has been freely associating with playful imagery is primed to tackle new ideas. Fantasy play, rather than being a distraction, helps children achieve the goal of having an open mind, whether in the service of further storytelling or in formal lessons.

As I continued to record the children's dialogues, my own mind began to open. I felt ready to risk the role of storyteller. Even now I can trace the path that led me directly from the children's play to a story of my own.

"I'm not Peter anymore and you're not the mother" was the statement from the doll corner that caught my attention. "Why not?" asked the presumed mother. "Because you'd rather be Jack? You could climb the beanstalk, okay?"

Neither Peter nor Jack would do; the plot had been derailed by more private concerns. "I'm angry you didn't let me stay home."

"I didn't say . . ."

"You want me to go away."

"No, you can stay home and I'll play with you," said the mother sweetly, and I knew I had a story to tell, one that would be true to the children and also to myself.

"Peter Rabbit did not want to go to school," I said, gathering the children on the rug. "He had not even realized that he was *expected* to go to school. His mother told him about school one day as she and Peter walked in the woods.

"Mother Rabbit pointed to the tall oaks and said, 'Mrs. Owl thinks you will be ready for school when the leaves turn yellow and begin to fall.'" Almost as one child, the children turned to look at our own nearly bare maples.

"Peter gave the leaves of the tall oaks a worried look. He wanted to stay home with his mother and his little sisters. 'But Mama,' he said, 'I can't go to school. They don't know what I look like.'

"'They will see you, dear child, and then they will know,' said Mrs. Rabbit. But Peter was not sure he belonged in a place called school.

"'I can't go to school, Mama,' he said again, 'because they don't know my name.' His mother smiled and nuzzled Peter with her warm nose. 'We will tell the children you are called Peter Rabbit and then they will know your name.'

"Peter and his mother walked along and walked along and then Peter said, 'But Mama, I don't know what the teacher does in school or what the children do.' Luckily his mother knew. 'One thing Mrs. Owl does is tell stories,' she said, 'and another thing she does is help the children play together.'

"Peter had one more question on this walk. It was harder to ask and he almost didn't ask it. 'Mama, do they know about Mr. McGregor?'

"'Ah, Mr. McGregor,' said Peter's mother. 'That was a scary time. He was chasing you and you had to hide in the watering can. You'll be able to tell them all about that if you wish. The other children will have stories to tell you too.'"

The children wanted to know whether Peter decided to go to school. "Did the leaves fall down?" they asked. "Is there going to be Mr. McGregor?"

"Peter definitely goes to school. But I haven't made up my mind about Mr. McGregor. I might just leave him in Beatrix Potter's book about Peter Rabbit and not put him in my story."

"Or Mrs. Owl could see him peeking in the window," a boy called out, "and chase him away."

How easily the children moved between the layers of my narrative, Beatrix Potter's, and their own. Years later, after I had stopped using Peter Rabbit in my stories and had begun inventing my own characters, I would still make use of the voices of the children at play. When their dialogues mixed with the events in my own stories, as was sometimes the case, I would have the extraordinary sensation of being in rhythm with every child in the class.

My imaginary characters were no different from those that entered the children's play. Our fantasy characters became our confidants. We would talk and listen to them and tell their stories at will. They did not mask reality; they helped us interpret and explain our feelings about reality.

seven

frogs, kittens, and bad guys

When I return to Mrs. Ruparel-Sen's room, there is no sign of an exploding tower. The block area is now occupied by Snow White's castle and the frog has been given a more heroic role.

"Pretend you're a frog and you jump into a bad guy but you don't know it."

"Grab 'em!"

"He's stealing kitty!"

"Get him, over there, get him!"

"Blast him, grind him up, he got the gold!"

"Meow, meow, meow."

"Here's your kitty, Snow White."

"Are you the dwarfs? The frog dwarfs?"

"We're the ninja dwarfs. The frog is a ninja. Watch out! We might have to blow this place up again."

Play may be the work of children, but we, the teachers, sometimes lose patience with what happens when the characters become too "heroic." In theory such play is fine, but the dramas that erupt can be loud and messy. By the mideighties we were trying to transform the children's work into projects and learning centers, hoping the players would not detect the differences. It made us feel more like real teachers when we controlled the topic, and we seldom borrowed our themes from the children's play.

Boundaries mean little, however, to frogs, kittens, and bad guys. Superheroes and princesses take their personas to the math table. "Pretend this is the gold and we bury it under the castle so the robbers can't find it," whisper the great pretenders, hiding the Cuisinaire rods under a pile of dress-ups. Somehow there was still an acceptable balance, in the seventies and eighties, between the teacher's illusions and those of the children, especially since no one demanded proof that we were getting a head start on reading and writing. We saw that the children were learning to play more effectively and that play, along with stories, music, dance, and art, provided the meaning and metaphor that flowed from one activity to the others. But the symbols of "real" work were competing with the children's art for wall space and the alphabet-as-art was being posted prominently.

Apparently one cannot tamper indefinitely with a magical kingdom. Large chunks of the neighboring first-grade territory shook loose and began to roll into the garden of children, depositing numbers and letters everywhere. The kindergarten teachers were distraught and felt helpless in the face of such knowledgeable adversaries. As the decade of the nineties began, fantasy play was fast becoming an endangered occupation.

Fortunately, certain basic traits in human nature do not easily yield to arbitrary changes. The children continued to enter school unaware of its plot to undermine their professional interests. "Pretend we're in school," they still say in Vijay's class, as they once said in mine. "And pretend we're sitting at a table and pretend we're looking at a book."

"But you *are* in school," Mrs. Ruparel-Sen tells them. "And you *are* sitting at a table looking at a book. It's *The Runaway Bunny,* isn't it?"

The children beam at one another for their audacious presumption. "We're pretending we are, right? And pretend we're bunnies inside this book," Jenny says, "and no one can turn the page because we're too heavy." Words, words, words, where do they all come from? It sounds like the poetry of a child's soul, nothing less, but the children are imagining a vivid drama that must be acted out.

"And no one can find us 'cause we're the real runaway bunny not in the book." They slip under the table but one voice can be heard clearly above the rest. "Except I'm the mother so I have to find you."

Nothing is remarkable about these conversations. Anyone who spends time with young children quickly recognizes their passionate attachment to fantasy and their need to alter time and place in rapid scene changes. Put any group of children together and they will make up stories that run alongside our own. It is an arrangement that has functioned well in the past. But today fantasy play is at the barricades with fewer and fewer teachers willing to step up and defend the natural style and substance of early childhood, the source of all this vocabulary building and image decoding and Socratic questioning.

Though fantasy propels the child to poetic heights over

and above his ordinary level and was considered the original pathway to literacy, it is now perceived by some as an obstacle to learning. We are allowed to nourish play only so long as it initiates reading, writing, and computing.

We continue to call play the work of young children while reducing its appearance to brief interludes. There is barely time to develop a plot or transform a bad guy into a hero. The educational establishment has ceased admiring the stunning originality of its youngest students, preferring lists of numerical and alphabetical achievement goals.

We who value play must do more than complain of unwanted drills that steal away our time. We must find time for play and keep daily journals of what is said and done during play if we are to convince anyone of its importance. Our children will happily join us in the project by giving us their stories that so well explain their play when the stories are acted out.

The children's intuitive resources have not been depleted. Every year a new army of adventurers enters the portals seeking promised treasures, bringing with them disguises and dialogues never before seen or heard or imagined. Welcomed or not, the children's thoughts run, flow, crawl, and fly into every corner of the classroom, marking out a pathway to learning. Their goals and ours can be a good match. They are, after all, making up stories and establishing rules, just as we do now and as we used to do when we were children.

At a faculty meeting, Elsie, a school counselor, recalls her own play. "My friend Mary and I found secret places where we could make up the rules. We played these scenes where we were big and tough and powerful, though we were just shy little five-year-olds. I remember every detail."

She has everyone's attention. Elsie has not been one to talk about herself in public. "I was Princess Gloria," she continues. "Mary was Prince Royal or the Green Ogre. When the sun went down, behind the coats in the cloakroom, where we were sent for whispering to each other, Mary turned into the wicked ogre. We had to keep tricking God so the sun wouldn't go down. We threatened to kill the angels and pull down the clouds and God always gave in and said He loved us best of all."

"But what did all that mean to you?" someone asked.

"That we were not little nobodies, I guess. We could create stories, any kind we wanted. The teachers were so indifferent to us. 'Cat's got your tongue?' they'd snap at me when I stuttered and couldn't answer a direct question, but then I'd be sent off to the cloakroom if I whispered to a friend. Mary and I figured we forced God to come to our defense by making up stories about Him."

The room grew quiet. Perhaps we were all trying to remember how it was when we were young. Something Elie Wiesel once said came to mind. "God created Man because He loves stories." And children, we might add, learn to play because *they* love stories.

eight

before there was school,
there were stories

When I was five, living in an immigrant neighborhood in Chicago, we stayed home and found our stories there. We created spaces and rituals in corners and under tables, listening to grown-up conversations at the kitchen table. We knew all the local shopkeepers by name and history and could walk to their stores by ourselves. We recognized the sounds of peddlers calling out their wares in the alley behind our building and ran to greet them.

The grocer invited us to pet the cat, and the fruit and vegetable man, the iceman, and the knife sharpener gave us sugar cubes to feed their horses. My friend Shirley called down to me from her third-floor back porch when she heard them coming: "Pirate ship ahoy!"

Like Elsie, the school counselor, I remember the fantasy play that held my days together. Shirley was the nurse, mother, or princess, and sometimes a spy, but I was Lady Annabella. The sugar cubes we fed to the horses contained magical potions that tamed them instantly, for they were fierce dragons waiting to devour us. We were five and not yet in school.

There were no television sets, VCR's, or computers to distract us and keep us and our families unapproachable for long periods. The radio provided a distant presence that did not demand our passive attention, and even "The Story Lady," who came on at five o'clock every weekday evening, could not take me away from play. By four-thirty my dolls were arranged around the living-room radio and I conducted my own classroom with Lady Annabella as teacher.

I hoped the Story Lady would be my first-grade teacher but, as it turned out, the teachers in my school did not tell long stories. Furthermore, Shirley and I had to leave Lady Annabella and the princess spy at home. School, in fact, was serious business, beginning as it did for many of us in first grade, but the three R's were not expected to interfere with opportunities to play.

There were morning and afternoon recess periods, and we all walked home for lunch. If we ate quickly, we had time to play again. After school we played until we were called in for supper. Even those of us who attended religious school several afternoons a week came home in time for play. "Ma, I'm playing something! I'll be right in!" could be heard from the courtyards of our buildings. The odd thing was, no one thought we played too much. It was what children were supposed to do, and when we didn't play our mothers would feel our foreheads to see whether we were sick.

There were stories we made up that engaged most of the younger children on our street and lasted over several days. Even those who took time to roller skate, play stickball or pinners, or run errands made an appearance in the play. "What part are you on?" they would ask. Older children, told to watch younger siblings, slipped into the role of judge or army captain. Boys and girls alike were frequently "in hiding" behind a bush, ready to jump on a horse and go after someone, guns blazing. When Shirley and I became tired of the chase, our doll buggies waited for us in the passageway next to the building.

By the midthirties, it was becoming commonplace to send five-year-olds to kindergarten. Miss Estelle, a kindly lady who played the piano and sang an octave higher than anyone else, asked my mother to keep me home until January, when I could enter first grade. The excuse used was that I didn't seem to like circle games and was shy with the other children. However, since Shirley's mother was told the same thing, our parents assumed that the school wanted to equalize class size, there being two entrance times in those days.

Lady Annabella and the princess spy were definitely not shy and were happy enough to remain at home. The school was apparently unconcerned about our readiness for first grade if we did little else but stay at home and play. Shirley immediately renamed herself Princess Alexandra and I decided to change from Lady to Princess Annabella so we could be sisters. Nothing less would do for the gift of play we had unexpectedly been given. "Pretend we're sisters and we live in a palace with a dark forest all around" was the way we began our daily play sessions.

"Pretend we're sisters" must be a universal longing of little girls and is still a favorite opening line in doll-corner dramas I observe today. Shirley had three sisters and I had none, but "sisterhood" had to be acted out. Decades later,

Princess Annabella and Princess Alexandra carried on the tradition in the stories I told to my kindergartners. "Pretend we're sisters and pretend we're picking blueberries in the woods," my characters often began, akin to saying "once upon a time."

As pretend sisters and royal persons, Shirley and I brought to life an assortment of characters who turned our private fantasies into social play. Edgar, a boy in our building who went to morning kindergarten, joined us in the afternoon after his nap. He was usually a scorpion going about stinging people, which Miss Estelle would not let him do in school. We allowed him to sting us in exchange for being a prince when needed.

Edgar's family spoke only Polish at home, Shirley's spoke Italian, and my grandparents spoke to us in Yiddish, but in play we shared a language in common. On the intimate landscape of make-believe we invented community and discovered one another's true identities. There were dozens of roles Shirley, Edgar, and I could explore at any given time. "Pretend I'm the teacher and I put you in the corner because you didn't do your homework. And then you try to sting me but I change into the wicked queen and then the prince comes to save us and I change into Princess Alexandra."

Years later in the kindergarten playground, the children seemed similarly preoccupied by this strange ogre called homework. "Do your homework this minute! Stop jumping around or I'll cook you in a pot and call the principal!" The children seemed to fly across the climbing bars, shrieking back at the pretend teacher. "We'll put a web on you and lock you in the dungeon!"

"Guess what?" I told the children. "I played like that when I was your age. A boy in my building liked to be a scorpion and also the iceman. He put the pretend teacher into a block of ice and sometimes she'd turn into a dragon so one of us had to be a witch to put a spell on her."

The children stared at me, disbelieving. "Who is the iceman?" they asked, choosing what was to them the least likely character in my story.

"The real iceman came in a wagon pulled by a horse. His wagon was filled with big blocks of ice that he carried up the back stairs into every kitchen. Up and down he'd walk, until we all had ice in our iceboxes. That was before we had refrigerators and we kept our food in an icebox."

"Were you Eskimos?"

"No, I was the same person then that I am now."

My story still seemed to lack context for the children. "Did you have dragons? Did you have Spiderman? He could spin a web over the iceman."

"Let's see. We did not have real dragons, only pretend like yours. I don't think we had Spiderman yet, but we had the Lone Ranger and his faithful friend, Tonto. They would have been on Spiderman's team because they were good guys. They rescued people." The children were satisfied and resumed their play, adding my iceman briefly to the plot.

Clearly it has not been the fantasy play that has changed over the years. However, our attitude toward the children spinning their webs during school hours is quite explicit. Stop your endless make-believe, we say. It is time to become real schoolchildren. Indeed, the children *are* pretending to be real schoolchildren, but they see a monster chasing them and so they must run into the forest and hide until their mother finds them and takes them home to play.

Fantasy play and its immediate connection to story-telling and acting are universally accepted by children. Howard, age six, in a Taiwan kindergarten, is introduced to storytelling and acting during my recent visit there. Chinese, of course, is the first language of the school, but Miss Lia comes in several days a week to teach English. She has noticed that, in play, Howard sometimes calls himself "bad bad Howard."

When my demonstration is over and I invite the children to dictate their own stories, his hand flies up. His whispered story, to Miss Lia, does not surprise her. "A bad bad Howard eats Miss Lia." She is pleased, in fact, for Howard has performed two feats of translation: from play to story and from Chinese to English.

A number of other children, ages three to six, tell their stories to Miss Lia, mainly in Chinese, which she translates for me into English. Then Howard rushes on to the pre-tend stage I have marked off with masking tape. He insists he must "finish" his story and proceeds to do so instantly, full-blown poetry, it seems to me.

"Dark dark Miss Lia and a dark dark tree,
Dark dark tree says 'go 'way Miss Lia,'
Dark dark Miss Lia goes away.
Bad bad Howard says 'bye-bye' to Miss Lia."

After the demonstration, Miss Lia and a group of teachers and parents gather to discuss what they have watched.

"I don't understand Howard's story," a parent says. "Is he showing hostility towards you?"

Miss Lia smiles. "I don't take it that way," she replies. "We've been reading an old folktale in which someone is lost in a dark dark forest. The idea of dark dark trees may have frightened Howard. Maybe he even imagines his teachers as dark dark beings and the classroom as a forest in which he might be lost, especially if he thinks he's been bad. So he puts these feelings into a story that seems like play. Now he can laugh at his fears. Don't you think his 'bye-bye to Miss Lia' is sort of a joke?"

The parent seems surprised by Miss Lia's interpretation. "But this is a very grown-up thing to do. Can someone this young understand how to do this? It seems like play, I know, but there is so much more to think about."

Miss Lia, who is herself a storyteller, tells the parents that she too has just realized how closely connected play and storytelling are. "When I saw the children acting out their stories I understood their play in a new way. We can't separate this play from the stories they learn to tell. And I think I must not separate both activities from my English lessons."

nine
big A and little a

Miss Lia and her students have time to explore the effects of play on storytelling, and the use of story in teaching and learning English. Formal reading and writing do not appear in Taiwanese schools before the first or second grade, though this is changing. She laughs and calls it "the American effect."

When did first grade lose its status in the United States as the beginning of formal learning? That was a time when kindergarten children were called the "little ones" by the other teachers who came by to watch them play. Even the older children recognized the difference between pretend and real schoolchildren. "Kindergarten babies, first-grade ladies" was the refrain heard on the playground, and there was some truth in the ancient tease.

Kindergartners were expected to be somewhat "baby-ish," and "immature" was a stage of growth and not an accusation when I began to teach. Yet, compared to nursery school children, the kindergarten girls and boys had entered the graduate program in fantasy play. The themes were lengthened and deepened and their conversations were more complex and analytical.

First-grade teachers approached their tasks slowly, knowing that their newest students still had one foot in fantasy play. "This is a big A," the teachers announced on the first day. "We'll do big A's for a while and then be ready for little a's." This was how the alphabet was introduced in first grade when I was a child and even when I began teaching in New Orleans in the fifties. The goal was seldom to teach the letter A; all the children knew their A's plus a few other letters as well. Some had begun to read on their own. But the display of the alphabet was the opening salvo of real school, where reading and writing would begin in earnest.

First-grade teachers were among the strongest advocates for the sanctity of kindergarten, warning us to stay in our own territory and not invade theirs. "Don't get into lowercase," they told us. There would be dire consequences, such as bad handwriting, nervousness, stuttering, and, in general, the self-defeating attitudes that often accompany the too-early introduction of formal lessons.

Behind kindergartners' attempts to write or read there were attributes, we were told, that we couldn't see and might misjudge, eye-hand coordination and aural discrimination being a few examples. And there were characteristics of kindergartners that were plain enough for everyone to see: restlessness, impulsivity, timidity, and a general state of dreaminess. The children themselves continually reminded us that play was still their most usable context. It was not the monsters they invented that frightened them in kindergarten; it was being told to sit still and pay attention for long periods of time.

Short attention spans were not yet considered a deficit in my schools in Great Neck, N.Y., and Chicago in the sixties and seventies. We saw that the children's concentration was intense when they played and we filled the other times with playful rhyming games, songs, and poetry, to which we added picture books and fairy tales. The children's own chants and shouts rang out as they ran, climbed, jumped, pushed, pulled, and rearranged their environment, all in the name of fantasy play. Restlessness, impulsivity, and timidness faded in the quest for a dramatic role, and daydreams awakened into social play and big arcs of paint.

There were faculty discussions in the sixties about the "new" superhero play. Did the growing access to television change the children's behavior? Now that Superman and Batman could be *seen* in action, was play becoming too aggressive? It was clear that the boys felt compelled to copy the look and sounds of every new superhero that appeared on television and in the toy stores, but the play itself was little different from the cowboy and army play of earlier generations and could be tolerated. Soon Barbie would arrive and the kindergarten girls did not take long to remake her into a mother, sister, or princess. In other words, little seemed changed in terms of kindergarten play and the opportunities it provided for expansive social interaction, innovative thinking, and endless subjects for conversation.

What we may have overlooked was the fact that young children were spending far more time watching television than ever they had listening to the radio. None of us imagined that children at home would voluntarily limit their own playing in order to watch television. We still took play for granted and talked about nearly everything else except its literary or philosophical potential. It was as if, in a discussion of library books, we spoke about the paper, the print, the bindings, and the cover, and ignored the stories that compelled the authors to write the books. Nonetheless, we found enough to admire in play to keep it center stage in classroom life.

Then, midway through the eighties and nineties, a new sentiment began to be heard. With the growth of nursery schools and childcare centers came the notion that there was too much play. Since children were entering school at a younger age, wouldn't they have had enough play before kindergarten? The need for play, in other words, was considered to be a factor of the number of early years spent in school. Furthermore, these early years were designated as the optimum time to introduce the shapes and sounds of letters rather than the shapes and sounds of characters in a story.

The principles of child development were being rewritten, unaccompanied by a huge outcry of disbelief. One began to hear the word "boredom" attached to play, probably for the first time in human history. It was an odd concept to tag on to the single activity children loved best, but there was a growing nervousness about what was going on (or not going on) in kindergarten. The "academic kindergarten" was offered as the antidote to boredom and, further confusing our logic and commonsense, children labeled "at risk," who often had less opportunity for play and talk at home, were allowed less time for these activities in school as well.

At educational conferences in the nineties, kindergarten teachers continued to defend play, even as they had to allow more and more paperwork to clutter the tables and walls. Some teachers tried to recapture the certainties of the past by collecting antique block sets and doll-corner cribs, ancient dolls, and little wooden cars and trains, resisting anything that came in a catalogue. But we overlooked the real villain in our midst. It turned out to be not so much the "academics" we were adding but the *time* we subtracted from the children's fantasy play that would begin to make the difference.

Having not listened carefully enough to their play, we did not realize how much time was needed by children in order to create the scenery and develop the skills for their ever-changing dramas. We removed the element — time — that enabled play to be effective, then blamed the children when their play skills did not meet our expectations.

Although we feared the influence of television, we were cutting down on the one activity that counteracts the mindlessness of cartoons. We blamed television for making children restless and distracted, then substituted an academic solution that compounded restlessness and fatigue. The children may have been the only ones capable of making sense of the confusion, and they did so whenever the schedule was cleared so they could play.

The misplaced academics of kindergarten affected the first grade as well. When kindergarten was the place for pretending school, first-grade teachers could take their time beginning formal lessons. It was always assumed that there would be ordinary children, without exceptional handicaps, who benefited from extra time to grow into academic areas. We called it maturation, and it was an important concept when we talked about children. Is it maturation or personality, we would ask when a child did not adapt to our activities? We were more inclined back then to look for fault lines in the curriculum than in the child.

We now have reversed the order of events. It is generally believed that the earlier we begin to train a child in reading and writing skills, the better off everyone will be. In many classrooms, the "pretend writing" of fours and fives looks real enough to begin keeping progress records. By the nineties a "chicken-and-egg" dilemma became apparent to me. Since the earlier we begin academics, the more problems are revealed, were the problems there waiting to be discovered or does the premature introduction of lessons *cause* the problems?

This conundrum does not exist in the abstract. Expectations for incoming first-graders are quite precise, and the tension begins even before the teacher and student meet. The potential for surprise is largely gone. We no longer wonder "Who are you?" but instead decide quickly "What can we do to fix you?"

ten

anxious families, philosophical children

One of the ways to "fix" these developmental uncertainties has been to hold children back. It is common now for nursery school teachers and families to doubt a child's readiness for kindergarten even if the child has impressive play skills. So many requirements have seeped down from the first-grade curriculum that it is hard to know how well a child will fare. In an effort to head off a crisis, an extra year of nursery school may be suggested by the teachers and parents.

In addition, the official entrance date to kindergarten has been delayed by several months, causing further confusion. The age span in a kindergarten class has widened, with the level of instruction geared to older students. Our five-year-olds are expected to know upon entrance the letters, sounds, and numbers that previously would have been a goal for the end of the kindergarten year.

We are somehow misplacing a year. The once clearly defined boundaries of kindergarten have lost their shape and purpose. "The children might as well go from nursery school directly into first grade!" a kindergarten teacher complained at a curriculum meeting. "No," replied a colleague. "In first grade we are doing what used to be done in second grade."

Families who insist on holding a child back cannot be blamed. Since the curriculum is often better suited to the older third of the class, parents and teachers are unwilling to place children at a possible disadvantage. Thus the decision is made to extend nursery school for some children. A curriculum, however, tends to take on a life of its own. With first grade dipping down into kindergarten, the higher expectations are shifted to nursery school. Lo and behold! The early childhood teachers are now trying to match their program to an arbitrary picture of what an older child needs. Be assured, no matter how the scene changes, play is given short shrift.

Indeed, there is little sympathy for a laid-back attitude toward any aspect of early childhood and decidedly less admiration for the idea that a rich variety of fantasy play represents intellectual growth. It may be that adult enthusiasm for the ingenious components of fantasy play will be relegated to the activities of two- and three-year-olds. Furthermore, we may have to look for such appreciation outside the confines of the schoolhouse.

Adam Gopnik, a writer for *The New Yorker* magazine, became fascinated by the fantasy life of his three-year-old daughter, Olivia. As he listened to her talk about her imaginary playmate, Charlie Ravioli, Gopnik pieced together a useful perspective on the hectic pace of urban life in New York City in a September 30, 2002, article called "Bumping into Mr. Ravioli."

It seemed incredible to him that so young a child could capture this modern-day dilemma in a few lines of pretend conversation. Here is Gopnik quoting his child. "'I bumped into Charlie Ravioli today,' she says, 'he was working.' Then she adds brightly, 'But we hopped into a taxi.' What happened then? we ask. 'We grabbed lunch.'" Later Charlie Ravioli cancels lunch, hops into other taxis, misses other appointments, and bumps into Olivia again, beginning the process anew.

Olivia's father quite properly saw his daughter's fantasy play as a brilliant commentary on the absurdity of certain contemporary ways. He may be forgiven for not knowing that Olivia's playful observations are typical of what one might hear from any group of young children at play as they create pretend characters and make up stories about them. If every classroom had its own Adam Gopnik to point out the significance of what the children say while they play, there would be enough material to fill *The New Yorker* for years to come.

Sometimes one word is enough to suggest a coherent philosophy. Fredrick, a three-year-old in a nursery school class of mine, once told me that the single word "Fredrick" was his entire story. This seemed insufficient to me. "What do you do in the story?" I asked.

"Nothing."

"You could go to school."

"No."

"Just Fredrick?" That was it, there would be no more. I asked the other children about Fredrick's story. "Is anything different?"

"Because he's Fredrick," Libby answered. She was four.

"The story has only one word, you notice," I persisted.

"It's not one word," said John, age five. "It's one person."

Of course. A person *is* a story. Everyone in the class understood that. Fredrick need not do something to justify his presence in a story or in a classroom. A dozen essays might be written on this theme; indeed it startled me enough to enter the philosophical position into a book I was writing at the time called *Mollie Is Three* (1986). Yet the children play out their "Charlie Ravioli's" and "Fredrick's" every day and seldom surprise one another.

They give themselves and others carte blanche to decide who to be: Fredrick frequently chose the role of robber or snake or the Incredible Hulk, but on that day he would be a boy named Fredrick. Similarly, Olivia has by now played her Charlie Ravioli theme many times, integrating its message into the fantasy play of other children. She may have decided to take up the role of a mom who always stays home and never hops into taxis.

Mr. Gopnik, as a professional writer, is trained to read between the lines, yet an anecdote sent by the mother of two-year-old Brian makes a equally interesting commentary on how young children "think," using the medium of an imagined drama.

"We were playing with scarves," Brian's mother writes. "I thought it would be fun to stretch a scarf across two stools and encourage Brian to crawl under, like a tunnel or cave. After going under the 'tunnel,' which is what I called it, he got his little bike and drove under it, saying 'car wash.' He was using play to go well beyond where I was, so I wrote down what he was pretending. 'Brian goes to the car wash.' He wanted me to read the sentence again and again while he rode under the scarf. It was perfect, the thought, the words, the actions, all Brian's. You could see he knew what he'd accomplished."

Brian and his mother had figured out a "lesson" together. Had other children been present they would have expanded the design. Olivia might have put Charlie Ravioli in the driver's seat, too busy to stop for a car wash. A year or two later the car wash might have washed her and Brian into the sea where they would suddenly grow tails. "Pretend we're a mermaid and a merman but someone ties up our tails and then Aquaman comes and he saves us." Aquaman, of course, is never too busy to save the day.

When our doll corners and other play areas are furnished with computers and charts, there may be too little time left for mermaids and mermen to escape danger and move on to new identities and adventures. Beatrix Potter and Margaret Wise Brown would worry about the new technical distractions in our children's lives, knowing that *Peter Rabbit* and *The Runaway Bunny* depend upon the imaginations of young children stimulated in fantasy play.

"Pretend Peter is hiding and Mr. McGregor can't see him. Not in the pot. He's crawling in the grass."

"Is he a baby? I could be a wolf with big teeth."

"No way! I jump up and I'm Super Rabbit!"

"I could be your big brother to scare the wolf, okay? And we scare Mr. McGregor."

The frequent deconstruction of Peter Rabbit in one class led me to inquire further. "Why is Mr. McGregor so mean to Peter?" I asked after a third reading on demand. "Couldn't he have given him just a small piece of lettuce?"

This is the sort of question children are eager to consider and the responses were quick in coming. "Mr. McGregor's afraid Peter wants to be his little boy and he already got enough kids," a child said.

"Peter eats too much" was another explanation. "Not just a tiny lettuce. Maybe he wants them all."

However, the third reply interested the children most and continued into their play when our discussion ended. "He thinks Peter is someone else he doesn't know. If he thinks it's Super Rabbit he'll be much nicer to him."

I tried to read their thinking. Is it safer to be a baby or a superhero? Both scenarios enlarged upon the original story, and any sighting of Mr. McGregor initiated further dramatization of Peter's dilemma.

At lunch, I brought the subject up again. "I noticed you were playing Super Rabbit before. But I didn't see Mr. McGregor."

"That's because Super Rabbit doesn't even eat the lettuce. He eats supercynide. That explodes you with super energy so you don't even care about Mr. McGregor."

When our concerns about academic progress in the early years causes us to minimize play, we may end up mourning the loss of many other worthy developments besides these philosophical permutations of babies and superheroes. At a conference recently, a kindergarten teacher reported on the gradual lessening of "ordinary niceness" in her classroom until she and the special education teacher decided to take matters into their own hands and reintroduce long play periods.

"This year we've included more 'special needs' kids in our room. These kids really have to play. They can't go from task to task like we sometimes do with the others, so their teacher would take them out for what she calls play therapy. All of a sudden this seemed crazy to me. *Everyone* needed play therapy. I convinced her to integrate what she does into the normal routine and now we work together to keep play as the central motivation and learning place, like in the old days."

The audience broke into applause, encouraging the speaker to continue. "Let me tell you, the kids are *nicer* to each other. At first we thought this was because we talked more about being kind to those who need extra help, but I really think it's something else. There is more time to be kind, to solve problems by playing in different ways, to include more kids and let them have a say."

"How do you get away with it?" someone called out. "What about the academic program?"

"Nothing's been removed. It's all still there. But we've discovered that less is more. And you know, the brightest kids make the most out of fantasy play. They set up a level of creativity the others follow. This kid Jeremy, for example, who's been reading for ages, started something in the blocks that involved all the Scooby Doo characters and Superdog and heaven knows what else. It caught on all around the room. Even Cinderella got into it. We've got an autistic boy who had not responded to a single activity yet—but he followed Jeremy around and put himself into the scene. We're pretty sure he was Superdog's rabbit pet. Everyone rises to the occasion, they're so happy to be able to play."

She had been speaking rapidly, as if there was so much she wanted us to know. But then she stopped and laughed.

"It's so satisfying, you know, just like playing in the back-yard when we were kids. There's a flow I remember, and a feeling that the world has slowed down enough for us to watch it turn."

At that moment the world did seem to slow down while each of us produced a vision of children, perhaps of ourselves, playing in some idealized backyard. Then a tall, dramatic-looking woman in a turban stood up and spoke to us.

"None of the children I teach have a yard to play in, not one where they are safe. They live in a project, not too different from the one I grew up in. But somehow I know exactly what you're telling us. That we have it in our power to slow things down enough to watch and listen to every child, to what they are saying, and take the time to say something back. Not because you're waiting for the correct answer, no. You want to hear them because they're telling their little make-believe stories, like children do in other places where they have safe backyards. I swear," she continued, "I never played one day in a nice backyard but I'll bet we can figure it out, the kids and me. Like when they keep after me to read the same story again and again, so they can stay with it and feel it deeper."

"Amen!" said the woman next to her. "The stuff we spend our time with doesn't go deep enough, does it?"

She fidgets with her rings, then stands up. "My name is Barbara. I'm at the same childcare center as Denise here, but I was luckier as a child. We did have a nice yard to play in, in our little Mississippi town. But more to the point is the fact that my mother and grandma were both school-teachers. Sure, we played the whole day long, but we also learned our ABC's and there was always someone waiting to read or sing to us and folks dropping by for long conversations."

She pauses, then continues, "I want to give these advantages to the kids in our center. They don't get to play enough, I know that, but they also don't get the verbal preparation at home. We just have to make up for that lack of stimulation and experience."

Barbara looks around the room. "Grandma always watched us play and talked to us about our ideas. Her sincere interest and curiosity made us receptive to everything else, even my big brother who was always restless and wanting to get away from anything that looked like a lesson. Grandma slipped in plenty of lessons, but it always seemed like we were telling stories to each other or playing games."

eleven

the art of conversation

Educators who feel that there is not enough verbal stimulation in an early childhood center may be able to identify fault lines without seeing the immediate connections to play.

A few years ago, when I asked a group of university mentors to a large Head Start district in Texas what aspect of classroom practice concerns them most, they were quick to answer. "Conversation! We don't hear good conversation. There are mostly one-line questions and answers, but the teachers don't simply converse with the children. And they don't encourage children to talk to one another, either."

As the professors gave examples of the sort of dialogues they overheard in the classrooms, it became clear that none took place during play. We agreed that conversation will be a frustrating goal if children's imaginative outpourings are removed from the equation. The more complex the thought, the greater is the child's need to view its meaning through play and find the characters and situations that bring ideas to life. From two-year-old Brian and his car wash to Olivia's harried Charlie Ravioli, the subject matter deepens year by year and the conversations grow longer.

"Peter Rabbit is a robber, you know," says five-year-old William, as Theresa, age four, pours two cups of tea. "But I don't think I drink tea if I'm a robber."

Theresa pushes a cup closer to William. "You could have it because it's chamillia-willia tea. That means it's for you because you're a *William*."

"But I'm a robber. They don't drink tea."

"Peter is not a robber. Oh, no."

"He steals the lettuce, so he *is* a robber."

"Mr. McGregor is mean. So it's okay for Peter to do that. And I'm your mother. You can't be a robber if I'm waiting for you."

This has been a conversation of great merit. The logic is clear: robbers do not have mothers who wait for them and give them tea. As to whether or not it is acceptable to steal from a mean person, the issue will arise again now that the idea has been introduced, stimulating new conversations. "William was wondering before if Peter Rabbit is a robber and if robbers drink tea," I might say during snack time. "And Theresa, you seemed to think Peter isn't really a robber, didn't you?"

Educators who wish to place good talk at the top of any literacy list are more than matched in this desire by the children's own intentions. The need to tell one another a story exerts a tremendous pull among children, powerful enough to overcome shyness and the fear of the unknown.

A father writes: "We've been trying to prepare our son,

Elliot, for his first day of kindergarten. But he's pretty resistant. He won't talk about it and won't even play the nice alphabet game we got him. Not even with his sister, whom he follows everywhere.

"Then, two days before school starts, he deals with the subject in a totally unexpected way. He tells his mother a story while she's ironing, plays it out really. It's all about school and his worries. It's a Beezus story, the character from his sister's *Ramona* book. This is pretty much what it sounded like:

"Beezus was not going to the playground. She was walking to kindergarten with her backpack. Beezus saw her teacher, Miss Joyce. Then Beezus got scared. (Of what? my wife asked.) She didn't know what scared her. The teacher looked furious. Beezus is running and everything is flying out of her backpack. And she hides inside the backpack.

"Quite a story, right? He got his sister to play it with him and at dinner he kept talking about school and Beezus and the teacher and the backpack. After that he seemed to be okay with the idea of school."

If Elliot is lucky enough to be in a kindergarten that revolves around play, his Beezus story will join the other fantasies in the room as the children confront the perils and possibilities of their new adventures in school.

twelve

who owns the subject?

The block area in Mrs. Ruparel-Sen's room is often the scene of dangers even greater than those Elliot imagined in his Beezus story, leading to a rise in the decibel level but also to good talk. Much as we take comfort in quiet playtimes, there is something about a fearful scene that often makes children more articulate and highly focused.

On this day, Kostos is shouting out directions to anyone who will accept the premises of his plot. Even Vijay is drawn into the drama. "Don't go there, Vijay! It's a poison river."

"Did my feet get poisoned?" Vijay asks.

"Don't worry, I'm making you invisible. Touch this paper. Now I got you unpoisoned. It's invisible writing."

"What does it say?"

"That you're invisible. No one can see you except me."

"That's good. I was almost dead."

"You mean poisoned. Now you're unpoisoned."

Life in Mrs. Ruparel-Sen's kindergarten is not without its scripted lessons and rote responses. The phonics curriculum, for example, provides a stark contrast to what we see and hear as the children engage one another in their play. After a busy session with "sh" words, the subject is dropped immediately by the children, who are eager to continue describing the poison river to one another and to the teacher.

"Do I see the poison if I'm invisible?"

"Sure you do. Only if you're not invisible then you step in it 'cause it sees where you're stepping. And you can use the invisible ink. Here!"

Vijay accepts the offer and uses his finger to write. "P-I. That spells poison," he says.

"Outstanding! P-I is outstanding!"

Mrs. Ruparel-Sen approaches the block area. "Did I hear someone say 'outstanding'? That's something I don't often hear in the blocks. What *is* outstanding?"

"See, me and Vijay got a great way to trick people. This sign says 'poison' but it's invisible ink so only invisible people can see it. Bad guys can't be invisible so they can't see it. So they fall into the poison river."

"How about me?" Shira asks. She is carrying a basket full of rubber animals. "I'm a zookeeper."

"A zookeeper? Touch this paper and you're invisible."

"My animals have to see me."

"No problem. Touch it two times and you're double invisible. No one can see you 'cept for the animals."

How well the children determine their new outcomes as the scenario changes. The whole point of this play seems to be the invention of stories about what could possibly happen. Dudley R. Herschback, Nobelist in chemistry, told the audience, in a 1989 conference called "Discovery," that the first thing he asks of his freshman students is to imagine the world before certain elements were discovered. They are to make up stories about such a world just as they did when they were children and always looked for a new story line when they played. And Kieran Egan, in his *Teaching as Story Telling* (1989), would have the teachers ask of themselves, "What's the story in this?" Whether in social studies, math, or any other subject, they and their students are to invent novel settings, plots, and characters in order to study ordinary phenomena from a fresh perspective. We must all be reminded, it seems, of what we did naturally when we were young.

The problem arises when the one activity in which the children can and do invent the story loses its legitimacy. Even the youngest children are capable of leading their teachers through the conversational byways of their own imagery.

During my visit to a childcare center, the teacher makes it clear that she knows who owns the subject in the doll corner.

Marni, a three-year-old, has been rocking an empty crib for ten minutes, humming to herself and glancing at a doll's arm visible under a pile of dress-ups.

"Where's the baby?" Mrs. Simon asks. "That crib is very empty."

"My baby went to someplace. Someone is crying." Marni stops rocking the crib and looks around. "Lamar, did you see my baby?" she asks a tall boy at the sand table.

"Yeah, she's in a dark forest," he says. "It's dangerous in there. You better let me go. It's down in this hole I'm making."

"Are you the daddy?" Marni asks. "Bring me my baby, Lamar. Oh, good for you, you found her."

"Was she in a dark forest?" Mrs. Simon asks.

"Where was she, Lamar?" Marni says. "Don't tell me in a hole. No, not in a hole, my baby."

"Not in a hole, no. Under a tree under a bush under a mushroom under a big rock." Lamar is a year older than Marni and moves easily through the various options.

"I'll say where," Marni decides. "Under a big rock name Ginger-head. Ginger-head is the rock 'cause it looks like Ginger. That's my mommy, Lamar. Ginger."

"Good," Mrs. Simon agrees. "Safe and sound under a rock named Ginger-head. And now I see your baby is safe and sound in her crib."

"Safe and sound, safe and sound," Marni sings, placing a shawl over the doll.

The conversation between Marni and Lamar reminded me of one held by George and Emily in Thornton Wilder's *Our Town*. Seated at a soda fountain, with a sudden sense of intimacy, George says, "So I guess this is an important talk we've been having."

Mrs. Simon must feel the same way, for she preserves the children's dialogue in her journal, intending to read it to Marni's mother at the end of the day. The family has been concerned about Marni's resistance to talking about school and her quietness in general. The events reported here would provide the same useful insights at home as in school.

Marni has another gift for her mother. "I did a story, Mommy," she whispers, handing her mother a paper. "Read it to me, Mommy."

"I'd love to, baby. 'The mommy and daddy carry the baby home. She was under the Ginger rock.'"

"Guess who's the Ginger-rock, Mommy! It's you! 'Cause you're Ginger."

The mother smiles at her daughter's new-found exuberance. It's only play, she might have thought, moments earlier. She will soon understand where the best conversations begin.

There are countless approaches to children's emergence as conversationalists. In a bilingual prekindergarten I visited recently in Houston, the children are encouraged to speak English during certain activities, but for play and story dictation they use Spanish. Their teacher tells me, "These subjects are closest to the heart. They will express their best selves first in their home language."

Jaime has been watching me since I entered the classroom. I think he would like to speak to me, but when I begin a conversation with him he looks away, embarrassed. Soon after I sit down opposite him at the story table, however, he finds a way, in his story, to establish personal contact. He accomplishes this by pretending I am acting out a scene with his mother. No one has taught Jaime to do this, except perhaps other children in the doll corner.

His first sentence is about a vampire and Spiderman, but his Spanish is too fast for me to pick up anything else. Then he says something that includes my name. "Jaime wants to know if he can put you in his story," the teacher says. "Yes, thank you, Jaime," I reply. Whereupon he inserts, in the middle of his vampire story, in English, "Mrs. Paley comes to my house. My mother says, 'Come in, please, and have some coffee! And then they talk together.'"

When it is time to act out Jaime's story, he tells his teacher that my part is first, before the vampire comes, and the teacher revises the script. "One day, Mrs. Paley comes to Jaime's house. 'Come in please,' says his mother. 'Have some coffee and we can talk.' They talk together.'" When my part is over, Jaime smiles at me and points to my chair. His story continues in Spanish and will not involve me or his mother, but the three of us have connected in an important way. When Jaime brings home his printed story, his parents may wish to talk about it further, for they have been made aware of the importance of storytelling and acting.

An older child may not need the dramatic intervention of play or of a story acted out with classmates in order to transpose experience into words. "Mom," he might say, "we had a visitor today and I really wanted to invite her over to visit you." Jaime, at age four, will *pretend* he invited the visitor to meet his mother in preparation for a later time when he has the ability to coordinate all that would be required to accomplish the feat.

thirteen
simon's story

Jaime's use of fantasy play and formal dramatics to bridge our language differences was straightforward and clear. But Simon, another four-year-old whom I met the year before in an Indiana Head Start center, has a more difficult task. He has been labeled autistic and it seems doubtful that he will join the storytelling activities I have come to demonstrate.

The children know Simon well, however, though he paces the room as if he doesn't see them. "What is Simon doing?" I ask Carly, who is about to dictate a story to me. "He's a zoo man," she says. Her tone implies that nothing is strange about the way Simon performs his role.

We watch Simon circle the room, punctuating his orbit with tiny cries and murmurs. His destination is a corner table under which a Lego zoo set awaits him, its plastic animals standing in a row. Once there, Simon crawls quickly to the animals and begins moving them across the tray, whispering to each one until they are all in place on the other side. Then he repeats his turn around the room and the process begins again.

"I think Simon is talking to the animals," I comment, and Carly nods. "Walk walk," she says. "He's tellin' them to walk."

There would be much for Simon to observe as he passes around and through his classmates' activities during "free-play," if he slowed down and looked. In the blocks, a space-ship is going up, and, next to it, train tracks tunnel under a math table and swing around the doll corner, where a noisy baby bangs on a crib yelling "Mama!" Family members come running, draped in layers of dress-ups and talking into Lego pieces held up to their faces.

Near the sink, children at easels paint large round faces while their neighbors coil long snakes on the clay boards. "This snake is poison," a boy warns one of the painters. "I'm makin' him a nest, okay?" the girl responds, painting over the smiling face on her paper with broad purple strokes.

Everywhere are the recognizable scenes and sounds of children making and doing and pretending together. A "Chutes and Ladders" game is crowded with players and onlookers; two tables of children negotiate the use of several rolls of masking tape for their drawings, paper cuttings, and armaments; a child at the computer receives advice from those waiting their turns. Simon weaves through them all and stops for none. His own activity demands his entire attention.

Anthony is next on the story list. "Mine is Dracula," he tells me and I print Dracula at the top of the page. "I wonder if Simon likes Dracula stories?" I ask. "Probably he does," is his reply and launches into his story. "This is Dracula and there is a dinosaur and they don't bite each other because they're friends." I can't help smiling. It's all about friendship: the play and the stories and the talk. But where does Simon fit in?

After several more stories, the children join me as I outline a stage with one of the rolls of masking tape. It may be the ripping of the tape that startles Simon, or the number of children crossing his path at once, but suddenly he is in our midst, stumbling through those seated along the edge of the tape. Back and forth he wanders, waving his arms until, with a series of shrieks, he returns to his appointed rounds.

"This is Holly's story," I say, holding up her paper. "She's a bird at the top of a tree and she'll need someone to be the tree, the mother bird, and a fish in the pond." The actors are chosen in the order in which they are seated, and the story-play begins. I get no further than "The baby bird flies to the tree . . ." when Simon again bursts on to the stage, grabbing Holly's legs while she continues to flap her wings, barely keeping upright.

"Simon, would you like to be a tree?" I ask anxiously, knowing there will be no response. Holly says calmly, "Simon is different." She places her hand on his head to steady herself and steps back into her story. She is not annoyed by Simon's behavior, nor are the other storytellers who follow. The actors carefully step over and around Simon, who now lies on his back moving his fingers across his eyes.

During recess, I remain in the room copying the children's stories into my journal. Silently Simon reenters the room and carries his zoo tray to the empty stage. I watch as he lines up the animals and I sit beside him on the rug.

"Walk walk walk," he instructs the bear and I add, "The bear walks over the hill."

Simon stiffens for a moment and glances in my direction. Then he moves the elephant through the blue patch of water and up the hill. His hand stays on the elephant as he waits for me to speak. "Walk walk walk," I say. "The elephant walks over the hill." By the time the children run in, Simon and I have together walked and talked to the lion, the giraffe, and the chimpanzee.

"Why is Simon doing his story now?" several children ask. "He brought his animals to the stage," I say. "They are walking over the hill."

The next morning, "doing stories" is one of many choices during free-play time. The story list fills up and I have no time to watch for Simon. Zoey, the second storyteller, requires my concentration. Her speech is hard for me to decipher and the only character in her story I am certain of is a "ki-ee-ca" (kittycat), because it meows. Fortunately the children at the table are familiar with her pronunciations and translate for me. "Can I be the frog?" Toby asks when the story is done, but Simon squeezes in beside Zoey before she can respond.

"Walk walk walk," he begins, placing the zoo tray on top of Zoey's story. He leans against us as he walks the bear to the top of the hill. "The bear walks over the hill," I say. Next come the elephant, lion, giraffe, and chimpanzee, and Simon and I act out his zoo story just as we did the day before. But this time he adds the wolf and he smiles.

In chorus the children at the table recite, "Walk walk walk. The wolf walks over the hill." Zoey's voice is the loudest.

fourteen
proving what we know

Sara Smilansky, the Israeli educator who pioneered in the study of play, had wondered why the children of certain North African immigrants to Israel had difficulty learning their new language. She wrote of her findings in many books, including her seminal work, *Sociodramatic Play* (1960). Much later she discussed her research at a 1992 conference on play at Wheelock College in Boston.

Smilansky discovered that many of the children were not familiar with the sociodramatic play that occurs spontaneously among preschoolers. It seemed to her that for the newcomers to risk a new language and engage in other school experiences, they must first learn how to play. The absence of play was a major obstacle in their path to learning.

Establishing a scale of play skills, Smilansky developed a method of peer-tutoring in which those who knew how to play "taught" those who did not. The skilled players served as models for those who placed lower on the scale. In the daily repetition of dramatic play, the children demonstrated the power of play as a learning tool.

As the less-experienced players gradually entered the world of play, they increased their language fluency and followed through on other concepts introduced by the teachers. Smilansky had shown a significant correlation between play and other measures of learning deemed important in a school setting. Her conclusions that play is essential and can be taught by peers to one another made immediate sense to the Boston audience. We were glad to have proof of what we already knew.

During the question period that followed her talk, Smilansky was asked how she would apply the peer-tutoring method in an actual classroom. Her research involved no more than six children at a time taken to a well-stocked play area in another room. Wouldn't the reality of a crowded classroom interfere with the smooth transfer of play skills?

Sara Smilansky's reply was honest and direct. "This is for the classroom teachers to figure out, not me," she stated. "I've suggested here that good play is taught by children to one another and it is probably the necessary precursor for every other kind of learning in a classroom. But this proof, if you will, must be questioned and put into action by every teacher who believes in play."

"Which comes first, a belief in play or the proof?" asked someone in the audience.

"I think faith in play is essential," Smilansky replied, "or you won't find the time to work out the proof." A good answer to a good question, we all felt.

The kindergarten and special education teachers mentioned in chapter 10 who combined forces were doing what Smilansky advised. They examined the effects of play upon a diverse group of children and proved for themselves how both inclusion and play advanced the common culture. They did not use the Smilansky play scale and may not have heard of it, but with a consistent comparison of events and the gathering of anecdotal evidence, they described to each other, day by day, the language, social behavior, and general creativity of the children. Perhaps they also kept track of the effects of doing less seatwork and having shorter scripted lessons. I wonder if they brought the anecdotal evidence of their study to their colleagues.

Teachers frequently establish "proof" of the effectiveness of their methods, not in order to write a dissertation or a book, nor even necessarily to convince others, but simply because once they discover certain truths, they can no longer teach in another way. The director of a pre-school in Taiwan, for example, explained her avoidance of punishment. "I used to have a punishment chair. Then I saw that, although the body was restricted, the child's mind entered many fantasies and behavior was never improved. I decided the approach does not work."

"Did you find what does work?" I asked.

"Patience. And then stories of good things happening, not bad. And making the child welcome into the play of others. I watched the children and saw that all these things work."

Sara Smilansky studied many areas of academic readiness; children are not one-dimensional, nor does their development proceed along a well-defined path. Everything we add to the mix along with play further advances learning. Drawing, clay, books, music, games, and dance suggest but a few areas of enrichment. However, it is the child's ability to play in a sustained manner that makes sense to other children, which opens the gates to all other pathways.

In dramatic play, language becomes more vivid and spontaneous, enabling young children to connect, with greater fluency and curiosity, the words and phrases they know to new ideas. The process involves not only the flow of words and imagery but of shared myth and metaphor, of knowing where the lost babies are and whether a dad can have sharp teeth like a wolf. "B is for bear" will teach the letter B, a good thing to know, but one must also know who likes to *be* the father bear and how bears and kittens might get across a poison river.

Furthermore, fluency is a reciprocal process, with teacher and student feeding each other ideas. There are teaching moments in children's play and stories that go well beyond "B is for bear." How do we extend the fluency of our teaching so that the art of teaching is in harmony with the art of fantasy play? How can the process even begin without belief in the potential of children's play?

Our visible support is required. When a poison river made of blocks begins to threaten the doll corner at its shore, we could complain that the blocks are taking up too much space or that the players are too noisy. This would not be inaccurate, for one set of children often moves to center stage and appears to be monopolizing the environment.

However, instead of dismantling the structure, we might suggest that a river can change its course and wonder if a bridge is needed to help the family in the doll corner cross the river to locate its lost kitten. Those in the poison-river scenario did in fact alter their plot and stage setting several times to include a bridge, a sea wall, and a princess in a silver boat. In addition, a zookeeper became "double-invisible" and a nonswimming aardvark floated across on a magic pillow. Children enjoy changing a story; pretending something can be different forms the basis of their fluency and can become the foundation of good classroom management as well.

Conversations with children may arise out of a "last straw" annoyance, in other words, or from a sense of dramatic flow. They can come from concerns over decorum or from respect for our imaginations. Both approaches will manage a classroom, but one seems punitive and the other brings good social discourse, communal responsibility, and may have literary merit.

My student teachers and I sometimes did our own pretending after school. We reenacted the altercations that had taken place and tried to imagine multiple ways of responding. Which comments of ours supported the play and extended the conversation? Which of our interventions dampened the spirit and spoiled the drama? What could we learn about fantasy play that had been unknown to us before?

When the children quarreled over space and materials, or entitlement and exclusion, we began to ask a new set of questions: Who are you pretending to be and what story are you making up? Problems that seemed unresolvable were often the result of a few details that no longer worked. Perhaps the numerical proportions of bad guys to good guys were wrong or there were too many runaway kittens compared to the number of sisters searching for them. It was little different from a similar disproportion in a math activity in which too many students had to share the manipulatives.

I brought this to the attention of the children one day. "There are five kittens in the doll corner," I pointed out. "The sisters are having a hard time with them. Are there too many kittens?"

"Me and Karen want them to behave. They only want to be bad all the time."

"We need a bear cub and not so many kittens!"

"The kittens are supposed to be waiting on the island for the queen. And then a swan comes."

The children seemed to have more options than I did in my math activity. It sounded as if new plots were being invented on the spot, exactly what happened when the children dictated a story. Smilansky's peer-tutoring came to mind, though in this case the plot itself was being doctored. In order to prove to themselves and to me that the script could work, the children were rethinking everyone's role.

Children will seldom sabotage their own plans if we give them a chance to find the way out. Bad guys turn into heroes and naughty kittens swim to an island, while a bear cub, a queen, and a swan are integrated into the story. The amateur playwrights in preschool are as eager as their Broadway counterparts to improve the play in tryouts.

A major difference between the two is that young children do not conceive of a final product or proof of achievement. They are always in Act One, on the first rungs of the ladder, preferring to linger there awhile. The children want to discover what the next question might be, before receiving too many answers from the grownups.

What is the question, one might wonder, for which three-year-old Amber has imagined the following answer.

She and Evan have just been sent out of a preschool doll corner after pulling at the same doll and shouting "Mine! Mine!" Having been told to choose another activity, Amber wanders around the room, stopping first at the easel to brush on a whirl of red paint, then moving on to flatten a clump of play dough.

Finally she comes to the story table. "Mine is about the tiger," she dictates when it is her turn. "And then the lion tries to eat the tiger. And the wind blows them over. And they was stuck together rolling and then they was friends again."

Was her question, how do I become friends again with Evan? When the story is acted out Amber insists that Evan be the tiger and the two children pretend to be stuck together, gently rolling back and forth until the teacher narrates the last sentence. "And then they was friends again."

"So the tiger and the lion got to be friends because they were stuck together?" the teacher asks.

Amber shakes her head. "No, first they was always friends," she explains. "And then someone thought they wasn't friends."

"Was that someone me?" the teacher asks.

Amber examines the teacher's face. "That someone wasn't playing in the doll corner, that's why."

Using the conventions of classroom drama, Amber and her teacher "prove" the potency of play to stimulate personal narrative and the art of focused conversation. Smilansky showed us that skilled players are the natural tutors for their classmates; Amber's teacher carries the process a step further as she enables Amber to work out a theatrical solution for a problem encountered during play.

fifteen

the subject was a puzzle piece

There is a powerful desire in any group of children to take up an idea, pass it around, and give everyone a chance to influence the outcome. This can happen in music and dance, in art and poetry, and extend into math, science, and philosophy. But the phenomenon appears first in fantasy play. More often than not, the children will focus on the most ordinary matters. On my next visit to Mrs. Ruparel-Sen's kindergarten, there is an unusual interest in a missing puzzle piece.

Four children have been playing in a "post office" built of big blocks and three sides of a cardboard packing crate. The two boys and two girls are posting letters to individual cubbies and working on a puzzle at the same time. The flurry of directives being issued back and forth comes to an abrupt halt when a problem is discovered.

"A piece is missing," they notify one another, glancing warily at their teacher, whose rule about puzzles remaining on the table is well known. "You brought it in here, Harry," Patsy whispers. "So what!" he snaps, but he looks worried.

"Anyway, I'm next on the list." He is referring to the story list.

Mrs. Ruparel-Sen soon calls his name and Harry slowly approaches the story table. Does she know? is written on his face. He hesitates while the teacher finds the next blank page in his notebook, then he blurts out the first sentence of his story. "There was a puzzle piece and it was lonely."

"A puzzle piece?" the teacher says, writing down Harry's words. Joni, drawing flowers at the story table, repeats "a puzzle piece," liking the sounds of the words.

"And it was lonely somewhere. And they tried to find another piece and another piece and a pretend 'nother piece, then it was all there. The end."

Joni looks up from her row of tulips. "What is a pretend puzzle piece, Harry?" she asks.

"You know, it's not really the right shape but no one notices and you push it in?" Harry's explanation is accepted. "Nice flowers," he tells Joni, as if in exchange for her interest in his story.

Harry's fellow conspirators have joined him at the table, adding their names to the list. "I'm doing a puzzle one," Patsy says, as Tarek sits down in the storyteller's seat next to the teacher. "Me too," he tells Mrs. Ruparel-Sen.

"Once there was a puzzle piece. Mine's not like yours, Harry. It's a golden one. And they had to find another one that had a sun on it. And the puzzle had one more to go. Then a boy came and there was only one piece missing. He saw a piece but it wasn't the one." Tarek stares at the page as if reading his teacher's writing. "Which word is 'piece'?" he asks, putting his finger where Mrs. Ruparel-Sen points. "I mean this *is* the one that's missing."

It must be clear by now that a puzzle piece is missing.

Mrs. Ruparel-Sen glances at the puzzle box on the block-area rug but makes no comment. Nor is she surprised when Patsy's story also refers to the mysterious puzzle piece, though it is somewhat disguised in a princess story.

"There was a princess and she sees a hole in the castle because a piece is missing." Having contributed to the general topic, Patsy develops her story along another path. "So then, two sisters came and one was seven and one was ten and their name was Hannah and Alexandra. One was in first grade and one was in second grade and they loved each other."

"Do the sisters live in the castle?" Mrs. Ruparel-Sen asks. "The one with the hole in it?"

"They *are* a princess," Patsy says. "That *is* the princess. Both sisters." Mrs. Ruparel-Sen adds this piece of information to the script and calls on Sarah, the final puzzle player. "Sarah, is there a piece missing over there in the blocks?"

"It is, but we're trying to find it. Can I tell my story?" The teacher nods and Sarah begins. "There was a princess in a castle and she went to swim and she did a handstand under the water and she sees a puzzle piece but it swims away. And her friends can't catch it because it swims faster. It's a swimming piece."

How does the fairly insignificant occurrence of a missing puzzle piece germinate so many stories? When they are acted out, those seated around the rug take the subject seriously, especially the part where the actors, as puzzle pieces, lie down on the rug, their arms and legs forming a close pattern.

I see on the wall a mural the children have painted of Leo Lionni's *Pezzettino,* the story of a small square that tries to discover to whom it belongs. It keeps asking larger configurations of squares if they are missing a piece. Has this fable provided the context for the missing puzzle piece? Is it loss in general that motivates the stories, or are the children anxious about the loss of this particular piece to a puzzle that was not supposed to leave the table?

Whatever the issues, the children's responses are not random. In following the trail of an immediate question that they alone have devised, they are also acquiring the habit of focusing attention on the many perspectives of a single idea, not too different from the way the story in a book evolves. Just as Pezzettino poses his dilemma to a succession of characters, the four puzzle players look for meaning in a series of skits. Pezzettino, of course, finds his answer at the end of the book. As for the children in their own stories, closure is not the goal.

I have known themes to evolve over several weeks in a preschool or kindergarten classroom, projects of the children's own making, accompanied by a persistence seldom seen in the activities we introduce. Curious to know if the missing puzzle piece would become such a theme, I called Mrs. Ruparel-Sen the following week.

"The outcome was different in this case," she told me. "With a little help from me, Harry traced the outline of the missing piece and I made a substitute one for the puzzle. By the way, remember Tarek's story about the golden piece, the one with the sun on it? Well, that is exactly the one that was missing. So we let him color in a sun. Once the puzzle was complete again, the stories about it ended."

In a Houston multilingual kindergarten, the subject in play and storytelling seemed to be *The Gingerbread Boy* on the day I visited. A variety of languages could be heard as the children played with the doll-corner oven, taking turns chasing Super Gingerbread Boy, but their stories were dictated in English. When appropriate, the teacher pointed to certain grammatical features of their sentences, but the practice seemed not to interfere with the children's intention to alter the plot of the traditional tale.

In the first story, a gingerbread boy helps his gingerbread mother bake a cake for his birthday and a gingerbread friend comes to the party. The next story has the gingerbread boy follow the original text, escaping from the oven, from a cow, and from a policeman, but stopping short of entering the river on a fox's back. "The end," says the storyteller before any harm befalls his hero.

It is the third story that directly confronts the expected ending: the fox eats the gingerbread boy, all but the head, which then rolls away laughing, "Revenge, revenge!" As the children dramatize the stories, each group of actors appears to grow in stature, as if a philosophical statement is being made: We have defined the subject; we have remained true to the subject; we own the subject.

There are times when the subject is owned by a single child. A four-year-old named Daryl in a Chicago public school prekindergarten class visualized *The Three Pigs* as "the wolf story." Later his teacher told me that Daryl often roars intrusively during playtime, telling children he's the wolf and he intends to eat them. Until she heard his story the teacher did not realize how vulnerable he felt in the role.

"A wolf story," Daryl began. "The bad wolf is on the roof. He falled off the roof because he was scared. He was scared because he hurted himself. And the pigs went on a walk on a rainy day."

"The pigs pay no attention to the wolf lying on the ground hurt?" the teacher asked. "They just go off on a walk?"

"They don't care," Daryl explained, "'cause they wasn't bein' hurt."

For Keta, another four-year-old in the class, the focus of her sympathy in a Power Puff Girls cartoon was not a trio of hapless little ducks but the river overflowing its banks. "Someone is crying," Keta said. "It's a river of water. It was making so much water no one could get on the stream. The water was making the river cry 'cause no ducks could swim there. The Power Puff Girls got them some puddles from the stream."

"Was it the ducks or was it the river that was crying?" Keta was asked when her story was acted out.

"The river," she replied. "It was so sad from having too much water so it couldn't get anyone to play there and it got lonely."

The prekindergarten teachers were impressed by the unique interpretations we were hearing. "Makes you wonder why these kids are called 'at risk,' doesn't it?" the head teacher asked. "But of course we've already understood how little that label really applies to these children. If you just listen to them you see how smart they are."

"Are you familiar with Lev Vygotsky?" I asked. "The Russian psychologist?"

The teacher nodded. "We studied him just a bit."

"Well, he could have been writing about Daryl and Keta, for sure. He said that in play a child stands taller than himself, above his age and ordinary behavior. It's as if he's climbing up a ladder and looking around at a larger area."

Vygotsky's image of young children standing taller, above their average behavior, as they pursue ideas in fantasy play, applies as well to their teachers who listen and try to make sense of the children's play and storytelling. The prekindergarten teachers who are curious and begin to ask about the children's easy inventions of a timid wolf and weeping river have begun to climb the ladder alongside the storytellers in their classroom.

sixteen
tom and jerry

The connection between Lev Vygotsky's words and a bunch of children running around pretending to be Tom and Jerry was not immediately obvious to me or my student teacher one year.

"It's become an obsession!" Gina complained. "We absolutely should not encourage these 'Tom and Jerry' stories." She openly disapproved of the cartoon cat and mouse who continually trick and hurt each other. "It's just violent, senseless drivel."

"Are *we* doing the encouraging?" I asked. "We sit there with deadpan faces while the children cheer for one character or the other." The Tom and Jerry craze had been going on all month and only the teachers resisted the daily event.

However, by the time eight children were regularly dictating Tom and Jerry stories, everyone realized there were a surprising number of ways the cat-and-mouse story could be told. With a quick alteration of text, the loser became the winner and cleverness triumphed over force. A ritual began whereby if one story favored Tom, the next one had to give Jerry the advantage. In other words, if Tom bit off Jerry's tail in the first story, then, as the stories were being acted out, the second story had to be changed to favor Jerry, literally rewriting the words of the story so that "Jerry pushed Tom out the window."

Gina was filled with admiration, in spite of herself. "I can't believe the kids came up with this by themselves," she said. "Like in Eddie's story today? Tom hangs Jerry out of the window ready to drop him into a thornbush when Angie reminds Eddie that it's Jerry's turn to win. So, instantly, he has Tom inviting Jerry to a birthday party. The kids even argue whether one action is *equal* to another, for heaven's sake."

"Have you changed your mind about Tom and Jerry?" I asked Gina.

"Not really. I'd rather no one watched these cartoons or any others. They don't need that stuff! But they *do* watch. I guess that's the point. And when they're allowed to include it in their play and stories, they *will* imagine other outcomes, it seems. Maybe sheer boredom drives them to it. After all, there isn't one kid in the class who isn't smarter than the cartoon characters."

"Does the bully issue enter any of this?" I asked. "Tom is the quintessential bully, isn't he? No one likes a bully and yet the children usually have some sympathy for him, more than the teachers do."

"Maybe they've figured out that under certain circumstances anyone can be a bully, such as with a younger sibling." Gina flips a page in her journal and writes something down, then looks at me with a flicker of embarrassment. "I'm doing a paper on Tom and Jerry."

She turns back a page or two. "Listen to this. Ellen figured out that if we arranged the Tom and Jerry stories in a win-lose order before we act them out, nobody will have to change the plot. So I thought I should ask everyone about that. Do they want to avoid changing the story or is that the whole idea, to *change* the odds for each character?"

Gina held her discussion the next day, tape recording it for her paper. Overwhelmingly, the children chose to stay with the original plan. "Because we like to be surprised," said one boy. But another objection to Ellen's plan was less easy for us to understand. "Don't mix up the notebooks," was one child's concern, "or you won't know what the story says."

"Do you mean we'll make a mistake when we put the story into the win or lose pile?" Gina asked.

"The notebooks will be mixed up. *They* won't know what pile they're on."

On the playground, I asked Gina what she thought of the final explanations. "I'm not sure," she said. "They didn't trust something about moving their notebooks around into a win-lose order, as if they would be losing control of their stories. Maybe it seemed too sleight-of-hand."

Gina ran to catch someone hanging from the parallel bars, then returned with a new thought. "I must remember this the next time I do a math lesson. Do the kids really see what I'm doing when I move all these rods and beads and cubes around? I mean, I shouldn't take for granted that when I pretend something—let's say, that each orange rod stands for ten white ones—that the kids make the leap in their imagination. They might be pretending something entirely different."

We sat watching the children chase one another around the playground. "The Tom and Jerry stories bring something else to mind for me," I told Gina. "Have you noticed that when the boys play Tom and Jerry on the playground, it's no longer just random chasing and grabbing? The alternate stories seem to suggest alternate play."

"The stories turn around and affect the play?"

"Well, usually we expect play to propel the stories, but the process works the other way too. It could become a good selling point. If the children's play seems chaotic, as many teachers complain, then storytelling and acting could be a way to improve the play. Anyway, it's something the teachers and children could study together."

By the kind of coincidence that frequently occurs when I zero in on a subject, soon after my conversation with Gina about the effect of the children's storytelling upon their play, I received another letter from the school director who had asked "Where has the dramatic play gone?"

Now she wrote: "Our inclusion teachers have begun the process of storytelling. They are at the point of writing down the stories and reading them to the group at the end of the day. So far they are not acting them out. Maybe they are afraid of too much emotion coming out. But I can see that the children are guiding the teachers and that the teachers are following. One child jumped up and began acting out his story while it was being read. It was quite spontaneous. But then another child did the same. The teacher said, 'Maybe we could figure out a way to do that with all the stories.' I think it won't be long before the connections to dramatic play open up. At least these two teachers have begun to honor the process."

seventeen

pretenses and perceptions

"Honoring the process" is a complex notion. We certainly try to do this when the subject is math or science, but to what extent do we transfer this seriousness of purpose when the subject is fantasy play and social behavior? In both these areas, our perceptions of what is taking place may differ vastly from the children's view.

I remember a boy named Steven who would sometimes report a headache, but only during playtime. Suspecting that the problem could be social rather than physical, I dealt with the matter almost as a politeness issue. Looking back, I wonder at the logic of my own behavior; apparently I valued closure then more than I do now.

"Those kids are giving me a headache!" Steven complained on one particular occasion.

"What are they doing?"

"Meowing! Right in my ear! It's not anyway supposed to be meowing in a spaceship."

The meowing had been audible throughout the room, but was not an unpleasant accompaniment to the cacophony of sounds in a kindergarten. Andrea, still in a red velvet cape, had crossed over from the doll corner where moments earlier she was a princess and was now a mother cat in the spaceship. "Tell them how you feel, Steven," I said.

"The meowing gives me a headache."

"Oh, sorry," the offenders said in unison, allowing me to resume my task at the art table. Andrea studied Steven while she licked her paw. "You wanna be the brother kitty?" she asked. To my surprise, he answered, "Can I be the baby?" and began to purr.

Why feign the headache if this was his desire from the start? The manner in which Steven achieved his goal was of no importance to Andrea. "Leo is the baby. You could be Baby Star Wars or Baby Ripley." He decided to be Wildcat Luke and immediately became the loudest of the several cats involved. It was only because my hands were full of clay that I decided to put off any discussion of the odd solution to Steven's headache and the part I was asked to play.

The children, however, did not find fault with my role. They expected me to maintain a polite society in which you do not give headaches, real or pretend, to others. They recognized Steven's headache as code for "they're leaving me out." It informed the teacher that something was wrong and served a useful purpose, in their view.

Within ten minutes, Steven was back with a new complaint about Andrea. "She knocked down my tower!" he pouted, righteous indignation replacing the headache.

"An accident, I'm sure. Is she still a cat?"

"Come with me, okay?" Steven was too distraught for me to argue the point. He took my hand and pulled me into the doll corner, where Andrea, minus the red cape and meowing, was now curled up in the crib. "Andrea, Steven has something to tell you."

"You broke my tower."

"Wa-a-ah!"

"Andrea, I must insist. . . ."

"Wa-a-ah!"

Steven's anger disappeared. "Okay, when you get bigger you can fix it. About three-and-a-half." Then he turned to me with the explanation. "She's too little now."

"She's too . . . ? Ah, I see. Babies can't build towers." I stood beside the crib, awakening to a new fact. I had taken a step up the children's ladder and felt elated, though not as much so as did Andrea and Steven. "But listen to me, Andrea. At cleanup, you must help Steven put away the blocks."

"Wa-wa," she nodded, staying in character. Steven sat down at a small round table covered with plastic food, watching Andrea. Then he brought a knitted coverlet to the crib. "Pretend I have to cover you up because I'm the dad and it's cold." Andrea looked up at him. "Da-da-da," she burbled, acknowledging his role.

In such little moments of theater, the children explained the logic of fantasy play. They were not asking me to suspend my views, but simply to take theirs into account. It seemed fair enough, but a few minutes later, in the face of a Star Wars explosion in the blocks, my newly acquired flexibility faltered and came to a halt.

"That's not Star Wars!" I shouted. "You are just dumping blocks!"

"It's not dumping," the boys protested. "Their X-94 rays exploded us. We'll build it up fast, okay?"

"Absolutely not. Too many dead people. We've talked about that."

"No, see, they come alive easy. We just need to spray this anti-94. Look! It's stored in this light saber."

Their logic was not different from that of the meowing cat or the crying baby, but I was unable to move forward with them. "It's really cleanup time anyway," I said in a kinder voice. I was not satisfied with the way I handled the matter but was relieved to see the blocks returned to their shelves.

Children are forgiving creatures. And Star Wars was not expected to go smoothly. The "explosion" itself may have signaled that an intermission was in order. In any case, plans were already being made for the next episode. "Can we have another playtime after lunch? If we do a perfect cleanup?"

I studied my advantage. "Let's see how things go. We've got a busy schedule today." But I knew I would try to accommodate the children. The feelings I had in the doll corner, of being in the right role at the right time, were still in place. "You know, your anti-94 spray did seem like a good idea. I guess you have to be prepared for all emergencies."

The boys' faces lit up. Their smiles came across to me with the force of a good evaluation from the principal. And yet I knew it was the sort of experience I would probably never discuss with the principal or with my colleagues. Perhaps this is why it seems so difficult to have a good conversation about fantasy play, in the manner with which a group of teachers might analyze a math lesson. Although, come to think of it, as Kieran Egan suggested, the math lesson would benefit from the inclusion of a bit of fantasy as well. Whenever we are reminded that there may be a story involved, our minds seem to loosen up and work better.

eighteen
what if?

From the earliest "pretend I'm the mama and you're the baby," play is the model for the life-long practice of trying out new ideas. Pretending is the most open-ended of all activities, providing the opportunity to escape the limitations of established rituals. *Pretending* enables us to ask "What if?"

I once heard a fourth-grade teacher say to his class, after a particularly aggressive game of four-square in the playground, "What if a kindergarten class came along and wanted to play four-square? You want them to have fun because they are so young and they trust you. So of course you want the game to be fair. Okay, describe exactly what the game would be like."

"Why are we doing this?" a boy asked.

"Because there is no trust in the game the way you play it. Four-square is a simple game, easy enough for five-year-olds, yet you kids can't seem to play it without ganging up on someone. You always make it three against one. When you were in kindergarten you were nicer to each other and you know it. Let's see if you remember some of that."

"Can't we just finish the game? It's almost time to go in!"

"No, I'm calling a halt to four-square until you can at least pretend to play with some semblance of fairness."

Returning to my classroom, I told the kindergartners what the fourth-grade teacher said. "I wonder why those boys were so mean to one another, or, should I say, mean to certain others," I commented.

"Because they don't like them?"

"Because they were mean first?"

"No, no, I know why. They're pretending to be bad guys, that's why. Now they have to pretend to be good guys." It seemed so easy in the kindergarten. Nothing was locked in place yet.

Not long afterwards I was able to make use of the What if? approach with a group of sixth graders. We were discussing problems of exclusion in the middle school and there was too much difficulty, I thought, in focusing on the feelings of the rejected ones.

A few boys had recently discovered Charles Darwin and were impressed by the idea of "survival of the fittest." The rights of the "stronger," also referred to as the "more popular," members of the class, and in particular, concerns for their privacy and self-determination, took precedence over all other considerations. It was a clear case of intellectual bullying by a few powerful leaders in the group, a sort of verbal Tom-and-Jerrying.

Remembering how the fourth-grade teacher tried to change his students' perspectives, I said, "Pretend you are lawyers. Your client is a sixth grader who has been discriminated against, especially in social activities and athletics. He hires you to represent him, not in order to collect a monetary award, but to make life in school more fair and just. What would you ask for on behalf of your client?"

The reorientation came so suddenly it was as if twenty cameras started flashing their lights at once. Arms began waving all over the room. Their teacher, Miss Hwang, decided to write down the first ten responses for further study, "before the jury goes out," she said. "Please speak slowly and distinctly," she added, "as a lawyer probably would." Then she began to print the new rules in capital letters:

1. OPEN UP EVERY ACTIVITY SO THERE CAN BE MORE PLAYERS.
2. DON'T TALK SO MUCH ABOUT WHO'S POPULAR AND WHO ISN'T.
3. STOP TALKING ABOUT PRIVACY. THIS IS A PUBLIC SCHOOL.
4. FIND OUT WHY CERTAIN PEOPLE ACT THE WAY THEY DO AND DON'T JUST BLAME THEM OR HATE THEM.
5. STAND UP FOR OTHERS. NOT JUST YOUR BEST FRIENDS.
6. FAIRNESS COMES BEFORE FRIENDSHIP.
7. DON'T CALL PEOPLE NAMES.
8. DON'T MAKE FUN OF SOMEONE.
9. SAY NICE THINGS TO PEOPLE.

"I'm putting on the tenth myself," Miss Hwang said. "If no one minds."

10. DON'T USE YOUR KNOWLEDGE OF CHARLES DARWIN JUST TO BE MEAN OR UNFAIR.

"I wonder how many of you will try to follow these rules?" she asked, stepping back to read them. I liked her no-nonsense approach.

"When *you're* looking, we will," a boy joked. "You're like the judge."

Everyone laughed, but the boy decided he was serious. "I mean we have to *pretend* we're being watched. Like those kindergarten kids on the playground? They keep yelling to their teacher, 'Watch me, watch me!' It's weird, really. They want to be watched all the time, just the opposite of us."

"Yeah, we just watch each other, then say something nasty," a girl said quietly. "Or some people do, anyway." Her words got everyone's attention and produced a sudden silence in the room. It made me want to tell a story.

"Long before Darwin, a Greek philosopher named Plato wrote a book called *The Republic*. It's all about his teacher, Socrates, who searched for justice and fairness and tried to figure out possible rules, just as you've done on the board. Now, one of Socrates' students, Glaucon, tells this story that seems sort of appropriate right now. See what you make of it.

"A magic ring is found that makes its wearer invisible when it's turned around. A shepherd gets hold of the ring and goes to the palace, pretending he's come to report the condition of the flocks. But once he's inside he makes himself invisible, steals the jewels, conspires with the queen to get rid of the king, and takes over the kingdom. The point Glaucon wants to make is that when no one is watching, people will take whatever they want and be as wicked as they can be."

"So if no one sees you, there's nothing to stop you?" Miss Hwang asked, expecting no answer.

"Then Glaucon goes even further," I continued. "What

if, he says, there were *two* magic rings. A just person puts on one and an unjust person puts on the other. Then what? Well, according to Glaucon, both people behave in the same way: badly. In other words, if you're sure you can get away with it, you're likely to behave unjustly."

"I don't agree!" An arm shot up and the speaker identified himself as Ira. "What if someone is being mean just because they don't want certain people to know they'd rather be nice? So then, if he's invisible, he'd act nicer."

"Yeah, Ira would, but hardly anyone else, I bet!" The boy complimenting Ira was the one who talked so much about Charles Darwin. He laughed, then said, "And my little brother would also. He's always telling me, 'You're not supposed to!'"

"Funny you mention your little brother," I remarked, joining the general laughter. "When my kindergartners invent an invisible person he can only be a good guy. Bad guys aren't allowed to be invisible."

nineteen
franklin in the blocks

Fantasy would seem to be nearly as useful a teaching tool in the older grades as in kindergarten. Children of all ages trust its logic and are willing to be moved by the power of its suggestion. In kindergarten, of course, it is the most reliable bridge between the children and ourselves since it is the passage they continually keep open.

My progress as a kindergarten and preschool teacher was defined and enhanced by the insights I gained into the children's use of fantasy as a learning device. Whenever, in fact, I myself used the power of make-believe in a new way, my confidence jumped "as high as the rainbow."

Take, for example, the case of Franklin, whom I wrote about in *Boys and Girls* (1984). The moment he entered the block area he made it impossible for others to play there. Until, that is, I decided to pretend he was a boy called Good Player. Looking back, I am certain that my response to Franklin in the blocks, as unexpected to me as to the children, changed me as much as any other event in my long career in the classroom.

The entire class had been affected by Franklin's outbursts. "Put those blocks down! Over here! No, leave that be! It ain't s'posed to go that way. Can't you just watch me do it? Give it here! That's too high! You're in my way!" Yelling and grabbing, listening to no one, Franklin managed to destroy all hopes of contentment in what to me was the most important part of life in the kindergarten. Even more than in the doll corner, the block area was the staging arena for communal learning. Accordingly, I always gave it the largest space in the room. Yet Franklin, single-handedly, was able to close it down in ten minutes.

His behavior came as a complete surprise, for he was skilled and helpful elsewhere. He showed children how to create careful constructions at the art table and carpentry bench; in conversation he was much admired for his knowledge of Star Wars and other fictions of the time. He welcomed anyone into his outdoor play, urging children to choose their own roles. "Who you wanna be? You wanna be a good guy or a bad guy?"

Then why was Franklin so unpleasant in the blocks? None of us could figure this out, though we all tried. "You're not the boss, Franklin! I had that first!" the children rebelled. "No fair! I'm telling! You're being mean! I hate you, Franklin!"

My assistant urged me to bring back the time-out chair, a punishment I had eliminated several years earlier. I had realized then that nothing good was accomplished by a time-out chair or any other means of removal and retribution. The Taiwan school director mentioned earlier had said it best: "I saw that, although the body was restricted, the child's mind entered many fantasies and behavior was not improved." Recall that when I asked her what did work, she added, "Patience first and then stories of good things happening. Not bad things."

My initial responses to Franklin were neither patient nor imaginative. "Look at what you're doing! You've made Teddy cry. He's trying to build and you're being very unfriendly to him."

"I ain't bein' unfriendly," Franklin defended himself, genuinely surprised at my accusations. "I told him he can help. But first I gotta show him how."

"Franklin's mean and selfish," the children said, and I could not disagree. Name-calling, however, did not convince Franklin, nor did my literary references. "Remember the fox in *A Blue Seed*?" I asked him. "The fox kept telling everyone to get out, get out, until finally the house collapsed. That's what you're doing, you know." The author, Rieko Nakagawa, must have had a boy like Franklin in mind, though Franklin objected. "I ain't the fox, no way! I'm sayin' come in, come in, soonest I'm done."

If not the fox, then who was Franklin pretending to be? A forceful, gruff bully of another sort? Since the business of young children is to pretend, and Franklin had chosen a role that did not suit us, why not suggest a more positive role for him? Hadn't I marveled at how quickly he'd switch from Darth Vader to Luke Skywalker on the playground?

When the class was assembled around the rug, ready to act out the stories they had dictated that day, I told the children I had a story of my own to do first and began immediately. "Once there was a boy who had a big problem in the blocks. Pretend I'm that boy."

After asking Teddy and Jonathan to bring a few blocks to the center of the rug, I began to wave my arms and shout.

"No, not that way! Not there, over here! That's not right! Watch me, give it here!" My behavior startled the two boys and everyone else but I kept it up a few moments longer.

Suddenly there came a roar of approval from Franklin. "That's me! You're pretending me, right?" He was laughing and pounding his knees. "Mrs. Paley's bein' me! Watch her the way she goes."

"You are absolutely correct, Franklin," I said. "I was pretending to be you. Okay, now I'm changing the story and I want you to be the boy. Once there was a boy who knew how to play in the blocks. He always let people build their own way. Everyone called him Good Player. Franklin, you pretend to be Good Player, will you?"

He bounded around the rug. "Hey, Teddy, put those blocks anyhow you want! I'll help you. How high you need this to go? I'll go get you some more, okay?"

The children squealed in delight. They realized Franklin was pretending, but my approach to the problem made sense to everyone. Did Franklin have a complete transformation? No miracles took place. However, when the old behaviors surfaced, we now had a useful story to bring up. "Hey, Franklin, you're pretending the wrong boy, remember?" He might begin to argue, then look around at the hopeful faces and laugh. Had he figured out that changing to Good Player was not too different than giving up Darth Vader to become Luke?

I asked Franklin once, "What if someone in *A Blue Seed* had told the fox he should pretend to be Good Fox who shares his house with all the animals in the forest?"

"Uh-uh," he answered. "That fox was too mean. That's too hard to change if you're *that* mean."

Franklin knew that he himself was never that mean, and the rest of us knew it, too. We'd had the opportunity to witness him in a great many roles. Franklin was also telling me, I think, that the issue is more complicated than our game revealed. When I described the event to a group of colleagues at a lower school faculty meeting, in fact, many teachers disapproved of my approach. "You just don't embarrass a child that way," someone said. "Copying his behavior in public is like making fun of him."

I tried to explain that the opposite effect is achieved. When children are enabled to see that they are playing a *role* and can easily substitute another role in its place, they are greatly relieved. *They* control the character; the character does not control them. I did not convince my colleagues, as I recall, but a few were curious. Perhaps they would one day try the method and find out for themselves how it plays out in a classroom.

Should I say "plays out" or "works out"? I decided to ask Franklin and his friends. "How can you tell if you're working or playing?"

"It has to be work if you tell us to do something," one boy said.

"How about when you make up your own stories? Is that work or play?"

"Play. Because it could be Star Wars or Superman. It has to be pretend anyway."

"When I pretended to be Franklin before, was that work or play?"

Franklin takes this on for himself. "That wasn't work *or* play. 'Cause you're the teacher. You was just teachin' us how we should play."

twenty
musical chairs

Every day brought me new evidence of the preeminence of fantasy in children's thinking. It has reinforced my certainty that we perform a grave error when we remove fantasy play as the foundation of early childhood education.

We are going too far in the opposite direction. Some school people feel that *because* young children engage in magical thinking we must pull them on to another track as early as possible; having added extra years of schooling to their lives, we are emboldened to counteract fantasy play with "reality-based" activities.

Is this not the adult version of magical thinking? To imagine that the purpose of early childhood education is to *reorder* the stages of human development is like the story of the prince who was turned into a frog. In attempting to turn children into creatures who are unchildlike, we ignore all the messages young children give us as they play. The frog turns back into a prince when the princess recognizes his need to be treated with kindness and respect. In the case of our children, this would include the kindness of acknowledging that their perceptions and premises are not the same as older children's or as our own.

Take the simple game of musical chairs. To one second-grader the game is "no big deal." He told me, "Look, first there's one chair for each player. You keep taking away chairs and end up with one guy—hopefully me—sitting on one chair. He wins, everyone else loses. See? No big deal."

Preschool and kindergarten children see musical chairs quite differently, I discovered. First, the game must be in the form of a story and second, no one is ever to be left without a chair. Evie, age four, having seen the game at a birthday party, brought it to Snow White's birthday celebration in the doll corner. The bursts of laughter from the five boys and girls marching around a play-dough cake drew my attention.

"Hi-ho, hi-ho, the dwarfs we go we go!" they sang, plopping down on chairs after each go-around. It was clearly a game of musical chairs except that every dwarf and Snow White always found a seat. Thinking I could add a touch of maturity to the game, I offered to show the group another way to play. "This is the way the older children play," I said. "It's the real musical chairs."

"This *is* the real musical chairs," Evie corrected me.

"I know, but may I show you another way to play the game?" I placed the chairs in a more orderly line and asked everyone to sit down. "Now, so far it's the same. But watch, I'm taking one chair away. The next time you march around one of you won't find a chair."

"Why?" several children asked.

"That's the fun of it, the surprise, you could say. Let's begin and you'll see how it works." Bringing back the chair, I sang several choruses of "Hi-ho" while everyone marched around, somewhat suspiciously. When I stopped singing there was a chair for everyone and the children relaxed enough to give a small laugh.

"Okay, now next time when I stop singing, someone won't find a chair, remember? That person can come stand by me." I again removed a chair and sang the song twice as the children cautiously moved around. I could see that I had made their joyous game into a lesson but it was too late to stop. "Hi-ho, hi-ho, the dwarfs we go we go! Okay, find a seat!"

Evie was left standing. "Where's Evie's chair?" Sam called out. "She's Snow White! It's her birthday."

I apologized to Evie and brought back the chair. "Sorry. I didn't mean to spoil the party."

"It's okay," Evie sniffed. "We're doing the next part now. Where the prince comes."

In September, the fives and I went on to kindergarten together. In the midst of an actual birthday party, the mother of the celebrant suggested a game of musical chairs. "We always did this at parties when I was young, Talia. You'll love it," Mrs. Gliddon said, offering to be in charge of the record player.

Mrs. Gliddon's enthusiasm carried the children around for two complete turns, with the losers solemnly position-ing themselves on my lap. But then Talia was the one who couldn't find a chair and instantly we were back to where we had been a year earlier.

"Talia can't be out," several children notified Mrs. Glid-don. "It's her birthday. No fair!" Suddenly aware of the in-justice, Talia burst into tears.

"It's not really unfair, darling," her mother said gently. "This is just the way it's played, you know." Talia nodded but continued to cry until her mother assured her the game was over and it was time for cupcakes. "But first, let's do the game once more with all the chairs put back, okay? Then you and everyone can find a seat." Talia hugged her mother and skipped over to her friends as if a great burden had been removed.

"But where's the challenge?" Mrs. Gliddon whispered to me as we placed the cupcakes on trays. "It seems so babyish for kindergarten."

Our student teacher, Anna, joined the conversation. "I think it's just not fun for them if anyone is left out. And anyway, pretending things is always better. This has been the amazing part of kindergarten for me. If I want the kids to pay attention I just say *pretend* we're going to do it and then we really do it. Pretend we're counting blocks, *pretend* we're lining up in the straightest line ever."

Talia's mother was doubtful. "Aren't you sort of tricking them?"

"It doesn't feel that way at all," was Anna's reply. "No, just the opposite. It feels like I'm respecting them. I'm taking into account how they feel and what makes them comfortable."

The next day, after dropping the children off in gym, I stopped into a second-grade classroom. "May I ask the children a question? Is this a convenient time?"

Assured that it was, I described the musical chairs game as preferred by the nursery school and kindergarten children. "Are you surprised?" I asked the students.

"Sounds boring to me," a boy said. "Doing it the regular way is no big deal, is it? Someone wins, someone loses."

"Yeah, for us, but not for little kids," a girl said. "My little brother, we always do things different with him so he won't think something bad is going to happen. Like if he's tired and we have to walk somewhere, we tell him pretend you're a puppy and we're taking you for a walk. Then he's happy. My mom got the idea from *The Boxcar Children*. The older kids, remember how they were so nice to their little brother, always pretending stuff and all?"

The girl didn't wait for me to offer an explanation. "See, you're *playing* with them." She studied her teacher, then looked around at her classmates. "Maybe it's hard to remember if you don't have a little brother or sister at home, but you're really incredibly *young* in kindergarten. See, we forget how it was, how many things scared us. Little kids have to be treated . . . uh, well, sort of like they're not really in school yet, you know. Then, in first grade, things really start to be different."

"How about in second grade?" the teacher asked.

A boy spoke up. "Yeah, we'd like to play more. It gets hard sometimes."

The teacher smiled. "I know," she said. "We really do need more time to play."

twenty-one
a letter from england

Trisha Lee is a London theater producer and director who has become intrigued by the play and stories of young children. "I sense the magic created in a classroom," she writes. "Sometimes the hush in the room when a child's story is acted out equals the spine-chilling feelings in an audience during a show in a big theater."

Miss Lee writes to me about her experiences as a drama teacher in a number of London schools where she uses the children's own stories as stage plays. "The other day a child in the reception class [kindergarten] in Myatt Garden (the school you visited) told me a story," she reports. "He had worked with me in the nursery class the previous year and knew the technique well.

"This is his story: 'Once upon a time there was a plane and he was going to crash into a building and make an explosion and all the people were hurt. And they got to die and then the firemen came and then the firemen put out the fire.'"

Her letter is dated December 5, 2002. Nearly fifteen months after the attack on the World Trade Center children continue to examine the explosion seen around the world. Whereas the "9/11" symbol may initiate discussions among adults, for children it will not suffice. They are compelled to communicate their feelings in more dramatic ways.

The letter continues: "When we came to do the story the children were totally engaged. I felt unsure, out of my depth, especially since the teachers didn't seem to expect the story. They had no idea the children were even aware of September 11th. Could we deal with this issue with five-year-olds? I worried about trivializing a serious event but decided to trust the child who told the story. He wanted to be the plane and he showed me where he wanted the building to be. He was very clear about the stage directions so we started acting it out.

"The boy, as the plane, flew to the spot where the building was and then gently curled up in a ball on the floor. I brought up five children to play the people. They took their roles of being hurt very seriously and when I read 'they got to die' they lay down in total silence. The room was hushed. Then I called up another five children as firemen who walked among the bodies of their classmates, holding hoses and putting out the fire. We all watched in stunned silence.

"It was the closest I've been to tears in the children's storytelling and acting. Then a girl asked, 'Can we do it again?' I said, 'I'm curious to know why you are so keen to do that story again.' She came and sat next to me and she said, 'Because it's really interesting.'

"So we did it again. Because the child was right, where I was confused. The children knew we had tapped into something really powerful, something that school and adults don't often let us tap into, a way of exploring our fears and the things we don't understand. But it also meant something else, that school was a place where you could feel very personally involved.

"For all my years in the theater and my belief in its value, I feel that right now I'm able to see its truest and deepest value. How amazing that this lesson comes from the age group listened to the least."

A few days later I read Trisha Lee's letter to a group of preschool teachers. No one doubts the authenticity of the children's voices nor is anyone surprised by the ability of fours and fives to enact the story in so respectful a manner.

"But what if they only care to do the violent parts?" a teacher asks. "Just the explosions and shooting and knocking things down? That's what makes me uncomfortable and I want to stop the play, and even the stories."

"Okay, but here's another what-if," I say. "What if you pretend you are a theater director and the children are your actors? And what if, having stopped the explosion, you say 'Once upon a time, what happened? Tell us exactly what happens before and after the explosion and what role you want to play. We'll get it all written down and talked about and let the story come out."

Our pretend theater director and her actors understand equally well that an explosion is merely a single event and "bang-bang" is not the whole story. It is not interesting enough. The what and the how of every story is deserving of our combined attention, determined visualization, and repetition, no less so in this tale than in the one about Cinderella or Peter Rabbit.

I bring the letter from England when I next visit Mrs. Ruparel-Sen's class and read the London boy's story along with the description of its dramatization.

The moment I finish, Kostos jumps up. "Can we do it?" he asks. "Can we do it just the same way as those kids? I really want to do that, okay?"

"Sure we can. Do you mind telling me why you want to do the story in the same way?"

Kostos considers my question for a moment, then spreads his arms and flies to the center of the rug. "Because it's really really interesting. And then next time, the firemen have to rescue the people, okay?"

The indomitable spirit of fantasy play lies in wait. When kept under the cloud of disapproval, as with any social, linguistic, or logistical skill, a period of practice may be useful. But the imagination is a dependable ally and the children's natural desire to tell a story, act in a story, listen to a story, and expand the story comes to the rescue. Then life in the classroom really becomes interesting.

In my next letter to Trisha Lee I describe the children's reenactment of her September 11th story. "Funny thing," she writes back, "how anything put into a story comes round back. So here's another one, also from a five-year-old, that shows how children see the world."

"'Once upon a time there was a bird. And he was flying around his nest and then he seed a tree what looked shiny. And then he called his mum and told his mum he seed a shiny tree. And then his mum told him, "There's no such thing as a shiny tree anywhere!" and he said "There is!" and his mum came to look. And his mum seed it and she told him "Let's pick all the shiny leaves off the tree." So they did.'"

"The image I found so strong was how the mum had not believed the bird and then when she finally sees the tree she had to pick all the leaves off so the shiny tree is no more. How easy it is for us to dismiss the children's play and stories as irrelevant make-believe and how children's creativity is eventually picked off by adults belittling and correcting till the child's tree is no more."

It is more than a funny thing, the way "anything put into a story comes round back." Once the storytelling habit grows strong it becomes a seamless process of invention and interpretation.

I can see Mrs. Ruparel-Sen reading the shiny-tree story to her children, who are eager to act out the roles of the little bird, the doubting mum, and the remarkable tree. Do the children wonder why the mother bird does not believe her child? And then, when she comes to inspect the tree, why is she determined to alter its most unique feature?

But these are *my* questions; the children will better recognize the secret twists and turns that help protect a child's fantasies from other versions of reality. How fortunate to be a teacher present at the creation and ready to carry on while the children revise and replay the endless possibilities suggested by a magical tree and a little bird who has the keys to the kingdom.